To ,X.   leg
            mig
Love,
Adele & Ray.

THE BEST OF RUTH PRETTY

PENGUIN BOOKS

Penguin Books (NZ) Ltd, cnr Airborne and Rosedale Roads, Albany,
Auckland 1310, New Zealand
Penguin Books Ltd, 80 Strand, London, WC2R 0RL, England
Penguin Putnam Inc, 375 Hudson Street, New York, NY 10014, United States
Penguin Books Australia Ltd, 250 Camberwell Road, Camberwell,
Victoria 3124, Australia
Penguin Books Canada Ltd, 10 Alcorn Avenue, Toronto,
Ontario, Canada M4V 3B2
Penguin Books (South Africa) (Pty) Ltd, 24 Sturdee Avenue, Rosebank,
Johannesburg 2196, South Africa,
Penguin Books India (P) Ltd, 11, Community Centre, Panchsheel Park,
New Delhi 110 017, India
Penguin Books Ltd, Registered Offices: Harmondsworth, Middlesex, England

First published by Penguin Books (NZ) Ltd, 2001

3 5 7 9 10 8 6 4 2

Copyright © text, Ruth Pretty, 2001
Copyright © photographs, The *Dominion*, 2001

The right of Ruth Pretty to be identified as the author of this work in terms of section 96 of the
Copyright Act 1994 is hereby asserted.

Designed and typeset by Seven
Printed by Condor Production, Hong Kong

All rights reserved. Without limiting the rights under copyright reserved above,
no part of this publication may be reproduced, stored in or introduced
into a retrieval system, or transmitted, in any form or by any means
(electronic, mechanical, photocopying, recording or otherwise), without
the prior written permission of both the copyright owner and
the above publisher of this book.

ISBN 0 14 301802 7
www.penguin.co.nz

THE BEST OF RUTH PRETTY

Ruth Pretty

PENGUIN BOOKS

INTRODUCTION

When I left school I wanted to be either an actor or a journalist, but eventually ended up as a chef, caterer and cooking teacher.

The penchant I had for acting has stood me in good stead as a caterer. At drama school I enjoyed learning the death fall, and at home would practise collapsing in a tragic heap and then come up smiling. Running a catering business has similarities to a drama school death fall – no matter what happens you can't stay on the floor. Improvisation was a big thing when I was at drama school. You were taught to build on the positive, always moving on to the next step of the story plot.

At the end of drama school the principal Nola Millar took me into her office to tell me the bad news. She said as there weren't many comedy parts for women, I shouldn't plan a career in the theatre. Little did I or Nola know that one day I would run a cooking school and students would attend for the comedy as much as the cooking.

I had always loved cooking, but never considered it as a career option. My mother was, and still is, an excellent cook. I love her stories of the tasty food her own mother cooked through the 1920s Depression years and the Second World War. She was the only sister sent to buy the meat because she knew which butcher to wait for and how to describe the beef corner cut so he would produce the best possible piece. And she knew how to smile appreciatively so that he always gave her a slightly bigger piece than what she was able to pay for.

My father owned a grocery store so we always ate well. My grandfather had been a baker and my father's great grandmother had been a caterer in Wangaratta, Australia. On 1 May 1889 the *Wangaratta Dispatch* gave a vivid description of a wedding Catherine had catered for, finishing with: 'Everything had been prepared in Mrs Osboldstone's most careful and elaborate style.'

When my mother shopped for food that wasn't stocked at the 'Apex' she specifically only ever ordered the best. She would ring Mr Chong for the 'best oranges', or Mr Cathiness for the 'best fish', and they would be delivered. Food was bought daily and the major purchase before the television was a small under-bench fridge.

My mother instilled in me that the quality of the produce you use is paramount to the standard of your cooking and that you have to be specific when you shop.

Anyway acting, writing and cooking seem to be somehow in the blood and have all melded into a most interesting career which at no stage I have ever planned.

Thank you to everyone at the *Dominion* who has encouraged me and helped with the column – in particular Richard, Alan, Simon and Ellen. Special thanks to Haana, who initially came to photograph our food as her first *Dominion* assignment and now photographs the column on a regular basis.

The recipes in *The Best of Ruth Pretty* have been selected from my columns in the *Dominion*. Thank you to everyone at Ruth Pretty Catering who amid the drama of a catering week have played a part in the column and this book – in particular Nicolette, Jacquie, Jo, Pauline and Shelley, and to Kirsten who has food-styled all the photos.

← Avocado, Orange and
Mint Salad

CONTENTS

← Smoked Salmon Mousse

01 Befores

Don't feel you always have to serve an entrée when you entertain. Keep guests away from the table with pass-arounds before the main event. Or try pass-arounds and then something 'suppery' instead of the main event.

Serve the vegetables you were going to accompany the main course with as a platter presentation before the main course instead of an entrée.

Serve 2 or 3 entrées instead of an entrée and main course.

Tapas

Tapas are appetisers that are served throughout Spain in bars and restaurants and are traditionally accompanied by sherry or other apéritifs. They can form an entire meal, and can range from simple items such as olives, cubes of sausage, ham or cheese, to more elaborate dishes, like frittata, stuffed peppers and bruschetta with toppings. Be generous with the toppings on the bruschetta.

→
Selection of Tapas (Bruschetta with tasty toppings)

Bruschetta

Bruschetta forms the base for many Tapas presentations. The fresher the bruschetta, the nicer it is.

1 baguette[1]
  (sliced on the diagonal into
  7mm to 10mm slices)
olive oil
crushed garlic (optional)
Maldon sea salt (optional)

+ Brush each bread slice with olive oil and toast on both sides under a grill, on a barbecue or on a grill pan.[2]
+ If you wish, rub with garlic and sprinkle with salt. Serve hot, warm or cold. Serve plain or with toppings.

NOTE: 1. For good bruschetta use Italian-style bread. Italian bakeries on this side of the world often name their long, thin sourdough loaf by the French name 'baguette'. 2. Bruschetta looks great with a criss-cross pattern achieved by cooking on a ridged grill.

Eggplant and Feta Cheese Paste

Spread thickly on Bruschetta and top with Pickled Mushrooms (see page 13). You could add a cherry tomato, left-over roasted vegetables or Italian parsley chopped with preserved lemon peel.

MAKES ENOUGH FOR 20–25 BRUSCHETTA

1 small eggplant (about 350g)
75g feta cheese
Maldon sea salt and freshly
    ground black pepper
lemon juice (to taste)

+ Preheat oven to 210°C. Roast eggplant until skin crinkles and the flesh is cooked. It will take 30–40 minutes.[1]
+ When the eggplant is cooked, open and scrape out all the flesh. Place in a food processor and process until smooth.
+ Crumble in feta cheese and process until blended.
+ Season to taste with salt, pepper and lemon juice.

NOTE: 1. You can also cook the eggplant on a barbecue. Put a metal skewer longways through the eggplant to make it easy to turn and cook until it is blackened and the flesh is cooked. This will give the paste a delicious smoky flavour.

Smoked Salmon Mousse

If you have any left over, try on hot toast for breakfast.

MAKES ENOUGH FOR 40–45 TOASTS

400g cream cheese
    (slightly softened)[1]
30ml (2 tblsp) lemon juice
freshly ground black pepper
¼ tsp Maldon sea salt
2 tblsp chopped chives
1 tblsp chopped dill
250g hot smoked salmon
    (skin removed, in chunks)
Vogel's Melba Toast
    (triangles or rounds)[2]

+ Beat cream cheese until smooth and creamy. Add lemon juice, pepper, salt, chives and dill. Mix until just combined.
+ Using a wooden spoon, combine cream cheese mixture and salmon (you do not want the mixture to be totally smooth).
+ When ready to serve, generously mound Smoked Salmon Mousse onto Vogel's Melba Toast. Alternatively, serve it in a bowl and let guests top their own toast.

NOTE: 1. You do not get a good result with low fat or easy spread cream cheese. 2. To make Vogel's Melba Toast cut bread, take crusts off and cook in 150°C oven for 40 minutes. Store in an airtight container.

Black Olive and Sun-dried Tomato Paste

Mound this paste thickly on Bruschetta and top with olive slices, a caper or shaved Parmesan. This paste also works well as an accompaniment to barbecued beef.

240g (1½ cups) black olives
    (pitted, roughly chopped)
95g (½ cup) sun-dried
    tomatoes (roughly chopped)
185ml (¾ cup) tomato sauce[1]
juice of 2 lemons (or to taste)
½ cup shredded basil (or ½ cup
    chopped Italian parsley)
Maldon sea salt and freshly
    ground black pepper
    (to taste)

+   Mix all of the ingredients.

NOTE: 1. We use homemade tomato sauce but you could use a good quality commercial variety.

Pickled Mushrooms

Add a bowl of Pickled Mushrooms to your Tapas presentation, or use as a topping for Bruschetta.

250g button mushrooms
    (trimmed)
500ml (2 cups) boiling water
1 tsp salt
500ml (2 cups) cider vinegar
6 peppercorns
½ onion (sliced)
1 sprig parsley
1 bayleaf
3 celery leaves
¼ cup olive oil

+   Cover mushrooms with boiling water and salt, allow to sit for 5 minutes and drain.
+   Set mushrooms to one side.
+   In a non-reactive saucepan, add vinegar, peppercorns, onion, parsley, bayleaf and celery leaves. Bring to the boil and simmer for 10 minutes.
+   Pour the vinegar mixture over mushrooms and cool.
+   Stir in olive oil and store in the refrigerator. To use, remove from liquid.

Skewered Thai Beef with Fresh Pineapple

These need to be cooked when your guests are ready to eat them. We often add basil to each kebab skewered between the beef and the pineapple.

→
Skewered Thai Beef with Fresh Pineapple

MAKES ENOUGH FOR 30 COCKTAIL SERVES

400g beef fillet
(trimmed weight)
Thai beef marinade
(see recipe below)
½ pineapple
salad oil
Maldon sea salt and freshly
ground black pepper
30 wooden skewers

+ Cut beef into 30 x 3cm cubes. Toss beef with enough of the marinade to just cover and leave for at least 3 hours. Reserve remainder of marinade for future use.
+ Peel pineapple, remove core and cut pieces similar in size to beef.
+ Drain beef of marinade.
+ When your guests are ready to eat, heat a heavy frying pan or a barbecue flat plate and smear surface with a little salad oil. Quickly cook beef cubes until medium rare to rare.
+ Remove beef to a bowl and cover bowl with a heavy teatowel, to rest beef for at least 5 minutes (this will ensure juices in beef are evenly distributed).
+ While beef is resting cook pineapple. Toss it around in the same pan you cooked the beef in.
+ Season beef and form kebabs by skewering warm beef with warm pineapple.

Thai Beef Marinade

When you have coriander to spare, make marinade and freeze. This marinade also works well on chicken or lamb.

⅓ cup soy sauce
1 knob root ginger (peeled
and roughly chopped)
1 tblsp brown sugar
1 tblsp fish sauce
small bunch fresh coriander
(stalks, leaves and root)
1 piece lemongrass (roughly
chopped)
1 red chilli (remove seeds if it
looks like a 'too hot' chilli)
1 garlic clove (peeled)

+ In a food processor with a metal blade fitted, combine all the ingredients.
+ Alternatively, finely chop non-liquid ingredients and mix with liquid ingredients.

West Coast Whitebait Fritters

Whitebait fritters remain one of our most asked for fingerfood items. People can't get enough of them. We also frequently serve (as an entrée or lunch dish) Whitebait Fritters with asparagus and Hollandaise Sauce (see page 46).

→

West Coast Whitebait Fritter with Asparagus and Hollandaise Sauce

MAKES 30 COCKTAIL-SIZE FRITTERS, OR 5 ENTRÉE SERVES

1 tblsp flour
2 eggs (lightly beaten)
250g West Coast whitebait
   (drained and gently washed)
salt and freshly ground black
   pepper
clarified butter (to cook in)[1]
juice of 1 lemon

+ Sieve flour onto beaten eggs and lightly whisk together.
+ Stir in whitebait and seasonings.
+ Heat a small amount of clarified butter in a heavy frying pan and using a teaspoon drop fritter mix into hot clarified butter.
+ Fry quickly on one side, only until egg mixture sets. (Do not wait for whitebait to go white.)
+ Turn fritter and quickly brown on other side.
+ Drain fritters on paper towels and squeeze lemon juice over fritters.
+ Season with salt and pepper before serving.

NOTE: 1. Clarified butter is great to use when frying (or barbecuing) as it doesn't burn.

Hipi Iti, Sun-dried Tomato and Pesto Sandwiches

We call these 'Prince Charles Sandwiches'. In 1994 I cooked dinner for Prince Charles at Premier House. With the drinks before dinner Prince Charles enjoyed this sandwich so much he asked me for the recipe. I heard later he frequently carries a black box with little sandwiches in it to sustain him when he is on tour.

MAKES 28 COCKTAIL-SIZE SANDWICHES

butter for buttering bread (softened)

14 slices white sandwich bread

about ¾ cup Sandwich Mayonnaise (opposite)

fancy lettuce

450g (5 rounds) Hipi Iti Cheese[1]

100g sun-dried tomatoes (finely chopped)

about ¾ cup basil pesto

+ Butter all slices of bread. Spread a layer of mayonnaise over half the slices and cover with lettuce.
+ Cut Hipi Iti into 4mm thick slices. Place 4 slices (in a single layer) on top of the lettuce.
+ Sprinkle the sun-dried tomatoes over the Hipi Iti.
+ Spread the remaining slices of bread with basil pesto and use to top the sandwiches.
+ Using an electric knife, remove the crusts and cut each sandwich into 4 triangles.
+ Store until required.

NOTE: 1. Hipi Iti is a ewe's milk feta cheese from Kapiti Cheeses.

↑

Cocktail Sandwiches: Hipi Iti, Sun-dried Tomato and Pesto Sandwich; Little Onion Sandwich; Roast Chicken, Herb Stuffing and Bacon Sandwich

Sandwich Mayonnaise

MAKES 2 CUPS

4 egg yolks
2 cloves garlic
Maldon sea salt and freshly
ground black pepper
1 tblsp wholegrain mustard
juice of 2 lemons
60ml (¼ cup) salad oil
440ml (1¾ cups) salad oil

+ Put egg yolks, garlic, salt, pepper, mustard, lemon juice and the first measure of oil into a food processor. Process until smooth.
+ Put the remaining oil into a jug and very slowly pour through the feed tube with the machine going.[1]
+ Taste for seasoning.

NOTE: 1. If the mayonnaise is too thick, slowly pour 3 tblsp of boiling water through the feed tube.

Spinach and Feta Cheese Fritters

These are an all-time favourite at Ruth Pretty Catering. Best cooked when you are ready to eat, but can be cooked ahead and reheated at 150°C for about 5 minutes.

MAKES 30 COCKTAIL-SIZE FRITTERS

2 tblsp flour
3 eggs (lightly beaten)
1 cup chopped, cooked,
squeezed dry spinach[1]
200g feta cheese (chopped
into cubes less than 1cm)[2]
Maldon sea salt and freshly
ground black pepper
freshly ground nutmeg
1 tblsp onion juice[3]
olive oil
1 lemon

+ Sieve flour into eggs and stir to make a light batter.
+ Add spinach, feta cheese, seasoning, nutmeg and onion juice.
+ Heat a heavy frying pan or a solid barbecue plate and smear with olive oil.
+ Using a dessertspoon drop batter onto hot cooking surface to form 3cm fritter. Fry until golden (approximately 2 minutes) on each side.
+ Squeeze lemon juice over fritters and season.

NOTE: 1. We use frozen spinach. You need lots of fresh spinach to achieve 1 cup. I like to keep fresh spinach to eat as a salad or vegetable. 2. If the feta cheese is too salty for your taste rinse it in cold water. 3. To make onion juice, grate an onion on the finest side of a grater or a microplane, and use the juice produced.

Crab Cakes

This recipe makes a big quantity so use what you need and freeze the remainder formed as Crab Cakes. We use Waikanae crab meat, which is available fresh and frozen in many fish shops. You could also use tinned crab meat.

→
Crab Cake with Tamarillo Chutney

MAKES 40–45 COCKTAIL-SIZE CAKES

500g crab meat
   (drained of any liquid)
½ red pepper (finely chopped)
½ yellow pepper
   (finely chopped)
1 red chilli
   (deseeded and finely
   chopped)
4–5 spring onions
   (finely chopped)
¼ cup chopped coriander
½ cup mayonnaise
1 egg
15ml (1 tblsp) fish sauce
15ml (1 tblsp) lime juice
½ cup fresh breadcrumbs
2–3 cups extra breadcrumbs
   (for rolling)
2 tblsp clarified butter
juice of 1 lime
Maldon sea salt and freshly
   ground black pepper
your favourite chutney
   to accompany

+ In a bowl, mix crab meat, peppers, chilli, spring onions, coriander, mayonnaise, egg, fish sauce, lime juice and first measure of breadcrumbs.
+ Form crab mixture into 3–4cm cakes and roll in remaining breadcrumbs.
+ In a large, heavy frying pan, heat clarified butter and brown crab cakes on each side (at this point you can freeze the crab cakes for later use).
+ Preheat oven to 180ºC.
+ When ready to serve, bake crab cakes in oven for 10 minutes or until hot right through.[1]
+ Season with lime juice, salt and pepper.
+ Serve with an accompanying bowl of chutney.

NOTE: 1. If you are using frozen crab cakes, you can thaw before baking but we cook them from frozen allowing an extra five minutes.

Parmesan Crumbed Eggplant Rounds with Roasted Red Pepper Mayonnaise

Our local growers laugh when you mention the culinary debate of whether to 'salt or not to salt' eggplant. Eggplant is salted to remove the bitterness and of course their eggplants are never bitter! Serve this dish as a fingerfood with drinks, or as an entrée. Great for vegetarian burgers.

MAKES 20–30 PIECES

2–3 eggplants
1 cup breadcrumbs
Maldon sea salt and freshly
    ground black pepper
¼ cup chopped herbs (parsley,
    tarragon, basil, sage or
    chervil, or a combination)
45g (⅓ cup) finely grated
    Parmesan
70g (½ cup) flour
3 eggs (lightly beaten)
olive oil for cooking
lemon juice
1 recipe Roasted Red Pepper
    Mayonnaise (see opposite)

+   Slice eggplants into 5cm thick rounds.
+   Mix breadcrumbs, seasonings, herbs and Parmesan.
+   Dip eggplant rounds in flour, eggs and then breadcrumb mixture. (If possible, rest crumbed eggplant rounds, in the fridge, for at least 1 hour before cooking. Layer with plastic wrap.)
+   Heat heavy frying pan, or flat plate of a barbecue, and cover with oil to about 2cm depth. When oil is hot, cook eggplant on both sides[1] and drain on paper towels. Keep cooked eggplant warm as you continue cooking.
+   Before serving, season cooked eggplant with lemon juice, salt and pepper and serve with a bowl of Roasted Red Pepper Mayonnaise.

NOTE: 1. Turn the heat to low and cook slowly so that the eggplant cooks through. These eggplant rounds are best cooked the day they are made. They also taste delicious cold.

Roasted Red Pepper Mayonnaise

This is also wonderful with crayfish. Try an open sandwich with crayfish medallions, Roasted Red Pepper Mayonnaise and thin strips of roasted red peppers.

MAKES 250ML/1 CUP

1 red pepper (halved and deseeded)
1 small clove garlic (peeled)
1 egg yolk
Maldon sea salt and freshly ground black pepper
½ tblsp lemon juice
dash of Tabasco
125ml (½ cup) olive oil

+ Grill pepper skin side up until the skin looks charred and bubbly. Cover with a teatowel and cool, peel and roughly chop.
+ Place pepper, garlic, egg yolk, seasoning, lemon juice, Tabasco and 2 tblsp olive oil into a food processor fitted with a metal blade. Process until smooth.
+ With the food processor still running slowly, pour remaining olive oil through the feed tube.
+ Taste for extra seasoning.

NOTE: If the mayonnaise does happen to curdle don't panic! Put another egg yolk and 1 tblsp water into a food processor bowl. Process briefly, then very slowly pour the curdled mayonnaise through the feed tube while the machine is still running. Roasted Red Pepper Mayonnaise can be made up to 4 days in advance and stored in an airtight container in the fridge.

Little Onion Sandwiches

James Beard, the American food writer, first wrote about these in the 1940s. Be kind to your guests and tell them if they end up with parsley on their teeth.

MAKES 30 COCKTAIL SANDWICHES

10 slices white sandwich bread
about ¾ cup Sandwich Mayonnaise (see page 19)
1 small onion (peeled and sliced very thinly)
Maldon sea salt and freshly ground black pepper
½ cup finely chopped Italian parsley

+ Using a 3.5cm straight-edged cookie cutter, cut 6 rounds out of each slice of bread. Spread each round generously with Sandwich Mayonnaise.
+ Place onion slices on half of rounds, season and use the other half to complete sandwiches.
+ Spread remaining mayonnaise onto a chopping board. Sprinkle parsley onto a plate.
+ Hold each sandwich lightly between the thumb and finger so that it will turn like a wheel. Roll edge of sandwich into mayonnaise, then into parsley.
+ Store until required.

Grilled Salmon Ribbons

These are very tasty little numbers, but have a receptacle at the ready for skewers. Ghastly to find them later in your colourful arrangement of flowers, foliage and fruit!

MAKES 20 COCKTAIL SERVES

400g salmon fillet
  (skin on, bone out)
oil for oiling tray
125ml (½ cup) soy sauce
60ml (¼ cup) fish sauce
1 tsp chopped mint
1cm piece fresh ginger
  (peeled and chopped)
2 red chillies (chopped)
1 clove garlic
  (peeled and chopped)
1 lime
Maldon sea salt and freshly
  ground black pepper

+ Slice salmon away from the tail into 20 thin strips[1] approximately 2cm wide x 8cm long, starting at the tail end and leaving the skin behind.
+ Thread salmon onto wooden kebab sticks (as if you were sewing a stitch) and place skewered salmon ribbons onto an oiled baking tray.
+ Combine soy sauce, fish sauce, mint, ginger, chillies and garlic. When you are ready to grill salmon, brush salmon[2] with soy mixture and place baking tray under a hot grill (you will not use all of the soy mixture so freeze for another time).
+ Grill[3] for 3–5 minutes until salmon is cooked.
+ Season with lime juice, salt and pepper before serving.

NOTE: 1. When slicing salmon ribbons from the wider end of the fillet, the strips may be too long so cut strips in half. 2. Beware of brushing the marinade onto the salmon any more than ½ an hour prior to grilling, as it will cause the salmon to break down. 3. If you wish, you can hot roast the salmon ribbons, rather than grill. Preheat oven to 230ºC and cook salmon for 3–5 minutes.

→
Grilled Salmon Ribbons

Roast Chicken, Herb Stuffing and Bacon Sandwiches

This is the ultimate chicken club sandwich. At Christmas time substitute turkey for chicken.

MAKES 20 COCKTAIL SANDWICHES

400g chicken breasts
olive oil
freshly ground black pepper
250g or about 9 slices bacon
   (finely chopped)
butter for buttering bread
15 slices white sandwich
   bread
about ¾ cup Sandwich
   Mayonnaise (see page 25)
lettuce of your choice
   (washed)
Maldon sea salt and freshly
   ground black pepper
1 recipe Herb Stuffing (sliced)
   (see opposite)
quince jelly

+ Preheat oven to 200ºC. Spray chicken with olive oil and place on a low-sided baking tray, season with pepper and roast for 15–20 minutes or until cooked. Cool, chill and then slice.
+ Reduce the oven temperature to 150ºC. Place bacon on a low-sided baking tray and cook for 10–15 minutes, stirring from time to time. Drain on paper towels, cool and then chill.
+ Butter all the bread slices on one side only and spread 5 slices with mayonnaise and cover with lettuce. Sprinkle bacon onto lettuce.
+ Spread mayonnaise onto another 5 slices of bread and place this bread onto bacon. Now butter and mayonnaise the upper side of those 5 slices and cover with chicken. Season.
+ Cover chicken with slices of stuffing.
+ Spread mayonnaise and quince jelly on the remaining 5 slices of bread to complete sandwiches.
+ Using an electric knife, trim crusts and cut sandwiches into quarters.
+ Store in the fridge until required.

Herb Stuffing

MAKES ONE 23.5CM X 13CM X 6.5CM LOAF TIN

120g butter
380g (3 small) onions
    (finely chopped)
900g fresh breadcrumbs
bunch sage and thyme
    (finely chopped)
6 eggs
Maldon sea salt and freshly
    ground pepper

+ Preheat oven to 210ºC.
+ Melt butter in a frying pan and sauté onions until transparent. Cool.
+ Add breadcrumbs, herbs and eggs to onions. Mix well and season.
+ Place into a sprayed loaf tin and cover with foil. Bake in oven for 40 minutes, or until firm. Remove and cool.

NOTE: For 20 cocktail sandwiches you will only use ¼ of this stuffing. Slice and freeze the remainder for future sandwiches.

Herbed Mussels in a Pot

We cook pots of mussels on the barbecue and place pots on tables so that guests can help themselves. Be sure to provide big napkins and soup spoons.

SERVES 3 TO 4

800g–1kg live Greenshell
    mussels[1]
250ml (1 cup) dry white wine
35g (2 large) shallots
    (peeled and finely chopped)
2 garlic cloves
    (peeled and finely chopped)
1 tsp Maldon sea salt
2 tblsp chopped Italian parsley
2 tblsp chopped chervil
45g (3 tblsp) butter (diced)
freshly ground black pepper

+ Wash mussels under cold running water. Remove beards (strings hanging from shell) and discard.
+ In a heavy-based saucepan combine wine, shallots, garlic and salt. Simmer for 5 minutes to slightly cook shallots and garlic.
+ Add mussels, cover and cook until all mussels are open. This may take up to 25 minutes.
+ Stir in herbs, butter and pepper. Serve in soup bowls with lots of the juice.

NOTE: 1. You can buy live mussels in tanks at supermarkets. Store them in the fridge and because they are live some will open, some may close. Mussels open as they cook. Discard any cooked unopened mussels.

Ricotta and Pesto Torte

←

Ricotta and Pesto Torte

This is one of our most sought-after recipes and is great to serve as you would a dip at a party. A client who had asked me for the recipe told me that she made this dish for her daughter visiting from Britain, who then asked for the recipe, made it for a business guest from New York, and that the guest's wife rang her from New York wanting the recipe. It's a chain letter recipe.

MAKES ONE 4-CUP BOWL

350g cream cheese
200g ricotta cheese
175g unsalted butter (melted)
½ cup sun-dried tomatoes
   (chopped if they are large)
½ cup lightly toasted pine nuts
100g pesto (rocket, basil or
   mint) (see page 71)
100g Sun-dried Tomato Pesto

Sun-dried Tomato Pesto made by processing:

2 cloves garlic
25g pine nuts
195g sun-dried tomatoes
½ cup Italian parsley
juice of 2 limes
½ red chilli or to taste
½ tblsp tomato paste
20ml reserved sun-dried
   tomato oil
Maldon sea salt and freshly
   ground black pepper

+ Allow cream cheese and ricotta to come to room temperature.
+ Process cream cheese until smooth. Add melted butter and process until combined. Add ricotta and briefly pulse to combine. Divide mixture into three as the torte will have 3 layers.
+ Line a 4-cup bowl with plastic wrap. Put a circle of sun-dried tomatoes in the base of the bowl and fill the circle with a single layer of pine nuts.
+ Spread the first layer of cream cheese mixture into the bowl and smooth with a spatula.
+ Cover this first layer with a thin layer of pesto and smooth with a spatula. Sprinkle half the remaining pine nuts over the pesto. Spread a second layer of cream cheese mixture and cover this with a thin layer of sun-dried tomato pesto. Sprinkle the rest of the pine nuts over the sun-dried tomato pesto.
+ Spread the last layer of cream cheese mixture. Chill for at least four hours before serving.
+ Unmould onto a serving platter and serve with Vogel's toast or plain crackers.

Curried Parsnip Soup with Filo Parmesan Biscuits

Many people have an aversion to parsnips that must go back to a bad parsnip childhood. Even non-parsnip lovers adore this soup. Try adding some pear with the parsnips for a change.

SERVES 8

90g (6 tblsp) butter
1 medium (about 180g) onion (peeled and chopped)
1 clove garlic (peeled and finely chopped)
1kg parsnips (peeled and roughly chopped)
15g (1 tblsp) flour
15g (1 tblsp) curry powder
1.2L chicken stock (hot)
150ml cream
Maldon sea salt and freshly ground black pepper
16 Filo Parmesan Biscuits (see page opposite)
chives to garnish

+ Melt the butter in a heavy-based saucepan. Add the onion, garlic and parsnips and stir to combine. Cover and cook over a gentle heat for 10 minutes (do not allow the vegetables to brown).
+ Add the flour and curry powder and cook for 2 minutes. Gradually add hot stock and bring to the boil. Simmer for 35–40 minutes or until the parsnips are tender.
+ Purée the soup in a food processor or blender and if you wish pass it through a sieve to remove any lumps.
+ Pour the soup into a clean pot and bring it almost to the boil. Add cream and heat through. Season to taste.
+ Serve soup in warm bowls garnished with chives and accompanied with Filo Parmesan Biscuits.

Filo Parmesan Biscuits

MAKES 16

60g (4 sheets) filo pastry
45g (3 tblsp) butter (melted)
40g (8 tblsp) freshly grated
   Parmesan

+ Preheat oven to 200°C.
+ Place a sheet of filo on a board and brush with melted butter. Sprinkle 2 tblsp Parmesan over the filo and top with a second sheet of filo. Brush the filo with butter and continue until all of the filo and Parmesan have been used.
+ Cut filo into 10cm squares and divide into 2 diagonally. Place on a sprayed baking tray and bake for 5–7 minutes or until pastry is lightly golden and crisp.

Bluff Oysters Kilpatrick

This is a very 'blokish' entrée and particularly good with beer. Unfortunately you can't often buy the prized Bluff oysters in the shell. Ask your fish supplier to source some shells for you or start a pressure group to return Bluff oysters to the shell.

SERVES 2

1–2 dozen Bluff oysters
120–240g rindless bacon
   (diced)
30–60g butter (finely diced)
Worcestershire sauce
Maldon sea salt and freshly
   ground black pepper

+ Preheat grill to medium.
+ Place 1 or 2 oysters in an oyster shell (or a small china gratin) with a dash of the oyster liquid.
+ Sprinkle bacon and butter onto oysters, drizzle with Worcestershire sauce and season.
+ Grill until bacon is browned. Serve immediately.

Val's Tamarillo Salad

This is a fabulous salad dish with cold roast pork, ham, barbecued lamb, or equally lovely with old-fashioned white bread and butter. One or 2 apples peeled and finely chopped and/or 1 cup shredded red cabbage makes a wonderful addition to this salad. The salad keeps well for up to 2 days, but add apple and cabbage just before you serve.

8 tamarillos (peeled)[1]
1 medium onion
  (finely chopped)
3 dessertspoons sugar
1 stick celery (finely chopped)
1 tblsp chopped parsley
your favourite vinaigrette[2]
Maldon sea salt and freshly
  ground black pepper

+ Remove stalks, chop tamarillos into small cubes and combine with onion and sugar in a non-reactive[3] bowl. Leave to stand for at least half an hour.
+ Add celery and parsley to tamarillo mixture. Drizzle with vinaigrette and season.

NOTE: 1. To peel tamarillos cut a cross at the base of the fruit, leave the stalk on, and plunge into boiling water for about 30 seconds. Remove from water, refresh gently under cold water and remove the peel. 2. My favourite vinaigrette recipe is ½ cup extra virgin olive oil mixed with 1 tblsp balsamic vinegar. Season with Maldon sea salt and freshly ground black pepper. 3. Non-reactive containers such as stainless steel, glass or ceramic don't react with the acids in foods. Tamarillos are very acidic.

$\rightarrow$
Val's Tamarillo Salad with white bread and butter

Fish Ceviche

This fish salad is delicious served in Cucumber Boats[1] as a passaround. As an entrée accompany it with Tomato Salsa (below) and iceberg lettuce.

← Fish Ceviche in Cucumber Boats

SERVES 4 TO 6 AS AN ENTRÉE

375g firm white fish fillets, (cut into thin strips)[2]
60ml (½ cup) fresh lime juice[3]
1 red chilli (deseeded and finely chopped)
1 large tomato (peeled, deseeded and finely diced)
1 tblsp finely chopped onion
2 tblsp diced cucumber
½ tblsp finely chopped fresh oregano
1 tblsp finely chopped coriander
Maldon sea salt and freshly ground black pepper

+ Combine fish and lime juice in a bowl, cover and allow to marinate in the refrigerator for 2 hours or overnight, or until fish changes colour. Stir occasionally.
+ Drain the fish of most of the lime juice but leave enough lime juice so the fish is moist. Add chilli, tomato, onion, cucumber, oregano, coriander and combine.
+ Season to taste.

NOTE: 1. Cut cucumber into slices approx. 7.5mm thick and using a melon baller make a round indentation in each slice. 2. We often use tarakihi. 3. The acid of the lime juice 'cooks' the fish.

Tomato Salsa

Serve with barbecued seafood or beef fillet, or fill avocado halves with Tomato Salsa and garnish with prawns.

MAKES 1 CUP

3 medium (400g) tomatoes (chopped)
1 large chilli (deseeded and finely chopped)
65g (½) medium onion (finely chopped)
½ tsp sugar
1 tsp lime or lemon juice
4 tblsp finely chopped coriander
Maldon sea salt and freshly ground black pepper

+ Combine all ingredients and stir to combine. Chill and taste for seasoning.

Tomato, Hipi Iti and Basil Salad

Buy tomatoes with the calyx on, this is the flavour seal. Use this salad as an entrée, or a lunch dish with crusty bread to mop up the juices.

→
Tomato, Hipi Iti and Basil Salad

SERVES 8–12

10–15 or so ripe red round
   tomatoes[1]
200–300g Hipi Iti Cheese[2]
extra virgin olive oil
balsamic vinegar
Maldon sea salt and freshly
   ground black pepper
handful fresh basil

+ Slice tomatoes in thick rounds and discard ends.
+ Slice Hipi Iti into rounds.
+ Alternate tomato and Hipi Iti rounds and drizzle to your taste with extra virgin olive oil and balsamic vinegar. Sprinkle with salt and pepper.
+ Tear some basil leaves and scatter over salad. Randomly stick sprigs of basil into salad.

NOTE: 1. I often use acid-free tomatoes for this dish. 2. Hipi Iti is a ewe's milk feta cheese made by Kapiti Cheeses. It is marinated in olive oil with herbs and has a mild, milky, slightly salty flavour.

← Orange Eggs Benedict

02 Weekends

Have a weekend day where you begin with brunch, late afternoon you take tea with homemade baking and much later have 'something on toast' for supper.

Crunchy Muesli

This is a recipe my brother John gave me many years ago. Delicious with yoghurt and poached fruit. I love it with preserved or macerated feijoas or Poached Tamarillos (see page 109).

→
Crunchy Muesli

MAKES 1.150KG – ENOUGH FOR 18–25 SERVES

100g sliced almonds
100g hazelnuts
100g currants
100g sultanas
100g dried apricots (chopped)
375g rolled oats
100g brown sugar
100g desiccated coconut
100g bran flakes
1 tsp cinnamon
1 tsp mixed spice
2 tblsp skimmed milk powder
250ml (1 cup) milk
15ml (1 tblsp) salad oil

+ Preheat oven to 180°C.
+ Roast nuts for 5–7 minutes or until lightly golden and skins can be removed from hazelnuts. Roughly skin and chop hazelnuts.
+ Mix nuts with dried fruit and set aside.
+ In a separate bowl combine rolled oats, brown sugar, coconut, bran flakes, cinnamon, mixed spice and milk powder.
+ Mix together milk and oil and add to rolled oats mixture. Stir until mixture is just dampened.
+ Place mixture in a shallow dish and bake for 50–60 minutes, turning the mixture frequently, until mixture is golden and feels dry.
+ Remove dish from oven and add roasted nuts and fruit. Stir to combine and allow to cool.
+ Store in an airtight container.

Betty Grables

In the 80s I owned a restaurant in Kelburn called 'Marbles' and this was a brunch favourite named by my restaurant partner, David Jordan. I know it sounds disgusting, but everyone loves it!

→
Betty Grables

TO SERVE 8

250g cream cheese
   (don't panic – you may not
   use it all)
16 slices toast-sliced white
   bread
160g raspberry jam
   (no other flavour works!)
160g thinly sliced ham
1 recipe French Dip
   (below)
clarified butter to cook in
icing sugar to garnish

+ Spread cream cheese thickly on one side of each slice of bread.
+ Spread raspberry jam generously on half the bread slices and place a slice of ham on top of the jam.
+ Place remaining bread on top of the ham. Remove the crusts from each sandwich and cut the sandwich into two triangles.
+ Melt a little clarified butter in a heavy-based frying pan or on a flat-plate barbecue. Dip each triangle into the French Dip and shallow fry on both sides in the butter until golden brown.
+ Drain onto paper towels. Sift icing sugar over the Betty Grables and serve.

NOTE: Delicious with a ripe peach half filled with sour cream.

French Dip

FOR 8 BETTY GRABLE SERVES

3 eggs (lightly whisked)
¼ tsp salt
15g (1 tblsp) sugar
250ml (1 cup) milk

+ Put all the ingredients into a bowl and lightly mix.

Corn Fritters with George's Guacamole

←

Corn Fritters with George's Guacamole

We often make tiny corn fritters and serve them as cocktail food garnished with a spoonful of George's Guacamole and a sprig of coriander.

SERVES 8

2 cups fresh corn kernels[1]
2 eggs (well beaten)
75g (½ cup) flour
Maldon sea salt and freshly
   ground black pepper
clarified butter to cook in
1 recipe George's Guacamole
   (below)
coriander to garnish

+ Finely chop corn kernels (you can use the pulse button on a food processor, but be careful not to over-process the corn as you do not want it mushy).
+ Combine corn with eggs, flour and seasonings and mix well.
+ Melt a little clarified butter in a heavy-based frying pan or on a flat-plate barbecue. Using a dessertspoon, spoon mixture into pan to form fritters.
+ Cook over medium heat for 3–4 minutes. Turn when golden brown and brown on other side.
+ Season with salt and pepper and place a dollop of George's Guacamole on top and garnish with coriander.

NOTE: 1. To remove corn kernels from cob, hold the corn cob upright on your board and scrape the kernels off with a chef's knife. These fritters are perfectly acceptable made with frozen or tinned corn.

George's Guacamole

My friend George is from Cuba and this is his mother's recipe, unlike any other guacamole recipe I have seen. It needs to be made just before you eat it.

2 ripe avocados
   (peeled and stoned)
juice of 3 limes
bunch fresh coriander leaves
   (finely chopped)
1 tblsp Dijon mustard
3 tomatoes (peeled, deseeded
   and finely diced)
Maldon sea salt and freshly
   ground black pepper
Tabasco (to taste)

+ With a potato masher, mash avocado with lime juice.
+ Stir in remaining ingredients.
+ Taste for seasoning.

Orange Eggs Benedict

Any sort of Eggs Benedict are great but I love the addition of orange. During asparagus season try Eggs Benedict with asparagus.

SERVES 4

1 tblsp butter
8 slices pork Kasseler[1]
4 pumpkin scones[2] (opposite)
8 eggs (preferably organic)
½ tsp white vinegar
¼ tsp salt
1 cup Orange Hollandaise Sauce
   (below)
1 tblsp mint (chopped)

NOTE: 1. Pork Kasseler is the eye of the loin which is cured, smoked and cooked. It is delicious also served cold. 2. You could purchase English muffins to use instead.

+ Melt the butter in a frying pan and brown the pork Kasseler on both sides.
+ Cut the scones in half and toast them lightly under a grill.
+ Fill a heavy-based frying pan with water and bring water to the boil, reduce to a simmer. One by one break the eggs into a cup and slide each egg carefully into the simmering water.
+ Cook eggs over a low heat for approximately 3 minutes, or until whites are set and opaque.
+ Using a fish slice remove eggs onto paper towels in a holding dish until you are ready to serve.
+ Place 2 scone halves on each plate. Put a slice of pork Kasseler, an egg and a dollop of Orange Hollandaise Sauce on each scone half and sprinkle with chopped mint.

Hollandaise Sauce

For Orange Hollandaise Sauce add the zest of ½ orange and substitute 1 tblsp lemon juice with orange juice.

SERVES 4–6

3 egg yolks
3 tblsp water
150g butter
   (melted and cooled)
2 tblsp lemon juice
Maldon sea salt and freshly
   ground black pepper

+ Put egg yolks and water into a heatproof bowl and place over a pot of simmering water. Whisk yolks until they are fluffy and light.
+ Very slowly add melted butter (not sediment or white liquid at the bottom), whisking all the time to ensure incorporation.
+ Gradually whisk in zest and juices, season to taste. Remove from heat and serve immediately or keep covered with a heavy teatowel for up to an hour.

Smoked Salmon Hearts

You can make sandwiches a day ahead if you store them in a tightly covered container in the fridge. Leave at room temperature at least ½ hour before serving.

MAKES 24 HEART-SHAPED SANDWICHES

about 75g butter (softened)
16 sandwich slices of fresh
    white bread
250g cream cheese
200g (32 slices) thinly sliced
    smoked salmon
1 lemon
freshly ground black pepper
    to taste

+ Butter bread and spread generously with cream cheese.
+ Lay salmon out and squeeze lemon and grind pepper on surface. Place salmon slices between two pieces of prepared bread.
+ Cut sandwiches with heart cutter.[1]

NOTE: 1. We use a 5cm-sized heart cutter.

Pumpkin Scones

We often make cocktail-size Pumpkin Scones and fill them with cream cheese, ham and quince jelly.

MAKES 6 SCONES

1 tblsp butter (diced)
100g (½ cup) castor sugar
¼ tsp salt
1 egg
1 cup cooked mashed pumpkin
350g (2½ cups) flour
2 tsp baking powder

NOTE: You can freeze scones uncooked. Make to the stage of cutting out rounds and place on greased baking tray and wrap well. Cook scones directly from freezer, allowing 1–2 minutes extra cooking time. Do not freeze raw scones for more than 1 week as they will form icicles.

+ Soften butter in microwave. Put butter, sugar and salt into a food processor fitted with a metal blade and process until mixture resembles fine breadcrumbs.
+ Add egg and process until pale and creamy. Add pumpkin and mix briefly.
+ Sift flour and baking powder onto pumpkin mixture and pulse for a few seconds until mixture begins to bind together (do not over-process).
+ Turn dough out onto a floured bench and gently press the dough into a disc. Roll out mixture to 1cm thickness and using a 7.5cm cookie cutter, cut into rounds.
+ Put rounds on greased baking tray and bake in a 225ºC oven for 12–15 minutes, or until golden brown and scones spring back to the touch.

Springfield Pear Cake

←
Springfield Pear Cake

We have a pear orchard of Packham Triumphs at Springfield and need recipes to use them all up. When this cake is just baked I like to serve it for dessert with Whiskey Sauce (see page 52).

230g (1½ cups) sultanas
250ml (1 cup) water
485g (3 cups) roughly
    chopped, peeled pears
125ml (½ cup) whiskey
1½ tsp baking soda
190g butter
240g castor sugar
2 eggs (lightly beaten)
1½ tsp pure vanilla essence
350g (2¼ cups) flour
1 tblsp baking powder
¾ tsp ground cloves
1½ tsp mixed spice
icing sugar for dusting

+ Preheat oven to 180°C. Spray a 25cm ring tin with baking spray.[1]

+ Place sultanas and water into a saucepan and bring to the boil over a low heat. Simmer for 3–4 minutes. Remove from heat and stir in pears, whiskey and baking soda. Cool.

+ Cream together the butter and sugar until light and fluffy. Gradually add eggs and vanilla, beating continuously.[2]

+ Sift together flour, baking powder, cloves and mixed spice. Spoon half of the dry ingredients and half of the pear mixture over the creamed mix. Stir gently to combine. Repeat with remaining dry ingredients and pear mixture.

+ Spoon mixture into prepared tin and bake for 50–60 minutes or until a cake skewer inserted comes out clean. Leave cake in tin for 10 minutes before turning out onto a platter. Serve cake hot, warm or cold, dusted with icing sugar and Whiskey Sauce.

NOTE: 1. Of course you can grease the tin with melted butter or oil but baking spray is so much more convenient. 2. This is the process where sometimes the mixture curdles. It is because the butter and eggs are at a different temperature to each other. If it happens ignore it and proceed.

Ploughman's Cake

I love this deep, moist fulsome cake given to me by Bunty Longuet.

TO MAKE 1 X 25CM ROUND CAKE

420g (3 cups) flour
1 tsp cream of tartar
½ tsp salt
225g butter
 (chopped and softened)
400g (2 cups) sugar
2 eggs (lightly beaten)
10ml (2 tsp) vanilla essence
10g (2 tsp) baking soda
250ml (1 cup) boiling water
600g (4) apples
 (peeled and chopped)
65g (12) pitted dates
 (chopped)
1 recipe of Topping (below)

+ Grease base and sides of 1 x 25cm springform round tin and line with baking paper.
+ Preheat oven to 180°C.
+ Sieve flour, cream of tartar and salt. Reserve.
+ Cream butter and sugar. Beat in eggs and vanilla to combine.
+ Dissolve baking soda in water. Slowly add baking soda and water to butter mixture beating as you add. Very quickly incorporate dry ingredients into butter mixture.
+ Add apples and dates and combine.
+ Pour mixture into prepared tin.
+ Bake cake for 1 hour then pour Topping over cake.
+ Bake for a further 20 minutes, or until a metal skewer inserted into cake comes out nearly clean.

TOPPING

125g butter
200g (1 cup) brown sugar
125g (⅔ cup) coconut
165ml (1⅓ cup) milk

+ Mix all ingredients in a pot and heat until butter is melted and ingredients are combined.

→
Afternoon tea of Ploughman's Cake, Smoked Salmon Hearts and Ginger Lemon Biscuits

Whiskey Sauce

I don't like whiskey generally but I love this sauce. If you have an ice-cream machine you can churn this sauce to make delicious ice-cream.

MAKES ABOUT 600ML

150ml milk
150ml cream
½ vanilla bean
  (split in half lengthways)[1]
4 egg yolks
70g (⅓ cup) castor sugar
60ml (¼ cup) whiskey

+ Put milk, cream and vanilla bean into a heavy-based saucepan and bring to the boil.
+ Whisk egg yolks and castor sugar until pale and thick.
+ Pour scalded milk and cream over egg mixture, whisking continuously.
+ Return custard to the pot and cook (over a gentle heat) until the mixture coats the back of a wooden spoon (do not allow the mixture to boil as it will curdle).
+ Strain the custard through a fine sieve.[2] Add whiskey and stir to combine. Chill until required.

NOTE: 1. Scrape the seeds from the vanilla bean and add with the bean to mixture. 2. You are straining to remove any egg white particles.

Ginger Lemon Biscuits

A crispy biscuit delicious with a cup of tea or as an accompaniment to a dessert plate.

MAKES 50 BISCUITS

115g butter
  (chopped and softened)
165g (¾ cup plus 1 tblsp)
  castor sugar
1 egg (lightly beaten)
1½ tsp (packed) finely grated
  lemon rind
½ tsp vanilla essence
160g (1 cup plus 2 tblsp) flour
1½ tsp baking powder
1 tsp ground ginger
¼ tsp salt
40g (¼ cup) castor sugar
  for sprinkling

+ Cream butter and sugar. Add egg, lemon rind, vanilla essence and combine.
+ Sift dry ingredients into butter mixture and stir until combined.
+ Wrap dough in plastic wrap, refrigerate for an hour.
+ Preheat oven to 165°C.
+ Using floured hands, roll teaspoonfuls of chilled dough into balls (approx. 2cm in diameter). Arrange on prepared baking trays (approximately 5cm apart).
+ Using a measuring cup (or any flat-surfaced object) flatten each dough ball to approx. 6mm thickness.
+ Lightly brush biscuits with water and sprinkle with castor sugar.
+ Bake for 16–18 minutes or until golden brown. Store in an airtight container.

Zucchini Cake

I first tried this cake in the USA at a Bertolli sponsored event. It has a simple method and is a great keeper – we used this recipe for a special project where we needed 2000 cakes. You may start with one cake!

TO MAKE 1 LOAF CAKE

225g (1½ cups) flour
150g (¾ cup) sugar
1 tsp cinnamon
½ tsp salt
½ tsp baking powder
½ tsp baking soda
210g (1½ cups) grated zucchini
130g (¾ cup) raisins
130g (¾ cup) sultanas
55g (½ cup) walnuts (chopped)
2 eggs
1 tsp pure vanilla essence
125ml (½ cup) olive oil
1 recipe Lemon Icing (below)

+ Preheat oven to 180ºC. Spray a 23cm x 13cm loaf tin with olive oil.
+ In a bowl, sift together flour, sugar, cinnamon, salt, baking powder and baking soda. Add zucchini, raisins, sultanas walnuts, stir to combine.
+ In another bowl, lightly whisk together the eggs, vanilla and oil.
+ Pour egg mixture over flour mixture and stir until just combined. Pour batter into prepared loaf tin.
+ Bake cake for approx. 1–1¼ hours or until a skewer inserted comes out clean. Allow cake to cool, before drizzling with Lemon Icing.

Lemon Icing

95g (½ cup) icing sugar (sieved)
1 tsp lemon zest
30ml (2 tblsp) lemon juice
5ml (1 tsp) olive oil

+ In a small bowl, combine all ingredients and whisk until smooth.

←
Beef Fillet wrapped in
Rainbow Chard

03 Main Event

Buffet presentations work for big crowds and when you want to maintain informality, but a buffet is more work for the cook. A buffet should consist of a few smart dishes rather than the multitude on a hotel smorgasbord.

Family-style presentation (I call it Italian-family style), where the food is plattered and platters put on the table so guests can help themselves, is my favourite way of having dinner at home, but you need to think carefully of table size – will everything fit? Consider the platters – will the guests be able to hold them to pass them around?

If you worry about guests not being ready to eat when you are ready to serve, remember many Mediterranean-inspired dishes taste as good or even better served warm rather than hot.

Potato Wedges with Sweet Marjoram

This recipe sounds weird but it works. As the potatoes soak up the liquids they become incredibly flavoursome and creamy, and crispy on the outside.

→

Winter vegetables: Potato Wedges with Sweet Marjoram; Roasted Stuffed Onions; Lemon-scented Broccoflower

SERVES 8

1.6kg large potatoes[1] (peeled)
250ml (1 cup) water
125ml (½ cup) lemon juice
125ml (½ cup) olive oil
3 tblsp freshly chopped sweet marjoram[2]
1 tblsp Maldon sea salt
¼ tsp freshly ground black pepper

+ Preheat oven to 220°C.
+ Cut potatoes into wedges and place in a non-reactive roasting tray. Mix remaining ingredients and toss with potatoes until they are well coated.
+ Bake potatoes uncovered for 30 minutes. Using a slice turn potatoes. You may need to add a little more water if the liquid has evaporated.
+ Reduce oven temperature to 180°C and bake potatoes for a further hour, or until fork-tender and brown on the edges.

NOTE: 1. We use Desirèe or Agria potatoes, but any large potatoes suitable for roasting would be good. 2. All marjoram and oregano are from the genus Origanum. Sweet Marjoram or Knotted Marjoram is the sweetest and most tender. In colder climates treat it more like an annual.

Lemon-scented Broccoflower

Broccoflower is a pretty green member of the brassica family – a cross between broccoli and cauliflower with a milder flavour than both. You can of course use broccoli or cauliflower in this recipe.

SERVES 8

zest of 1 lemon
30ml (2 tblsp) lemon juice
600g (1 head) broccoflower (cut into flowerets)
olive oil for spraying
leaves from 6 sprigs oregano
2 tsp Maldon sea salt
freshly ground black pepper

+ Preheat oven to 230°C.
+ In a bowl, mix together lemon zest, lemon juice and broccoflower, and spread in a single layer on a low-sided tray. Spray or toss with olive oil and sprinkle with oregano leaves, salt and pepper.
+ Roast broccoflower for 10 minutes or until cooked through and brown around the edges.

Roasted Stuffed Onions

For a wintry entrée exclude the vinaigrette from this recipe and top the vegetables with Gruyère or blue cheese sauce before you reheat. Use brown or red onions.

SERVES 8

4 large onions with skins on
butter for greasing tray
200g butternut (peeled and cut
    into 1cm dice)
200g red pepper (deseeded
    and cut into 1cm-wide strips)
200g yams (cut on a diagonal
    5mm wide)
30ml (2 tblsp) olive oil for
    cooking vegetables
Maldon sea salt and freshly
    ground black pepper
bunch thyme (squashed)
60ml (4 tblsp) vinaigrette[1]

+ Preheat oven to 200°C.
+ Slice onions in half widthwise and place cut side down on buttered tray. Cook onions for 30 minutes, or until they are brown underneath.
+ Remove onions from oven and increase temperature to 250°C. Allow onions to cool, then peel off outer skin and discard. Remove inner part of onion for later use. You will be left with an onion 'cup'.
+ Slice inner part and combine with remaining vegetables. Toss with olive oil, salt and pepper.
+ Place thyme and vegetables on a low-sided roasting tray in a single layer.
+ Roast vegetables for 10–12 minutes, or until fork-tender. Discard thyme. Pile vegetables into onion cups. Drizzle 1 tsp vinaigrette into each vegetable cup.
+ When you are ready to serve heat oven to 180°C. Place onion cups into oven and reheat for 5–10 minutes, or until heated through.

NOTE: 1. Mix ½ cup olive oil with 1 tblsp balsamic vinegar and season.

Spinach and Bacon Salad

Fresh, raw spinach is a great winter salad vegetable.

SERVES 6

10 bacon rashers (diced)
500g spinach (washed and
    stalks removed)
60 ml (¼ cup) The Most Tasty
    Vinaigrette (opposite)
3 hard-boiled eggs (peeled,
    mashed or quartered)

+ Render fat from bacon in a heavy pan over medium heat. Drain fat from bacon and spread bacon on a low-sided tray. Bake at 150°C for about 10 minutes or until crispy. Drain on paper towels.
+ Place spinach in a serving bowl, add enough Tasty Vinaigrette to coat and toss lightly. Sprinkle eggs and bacon on salad and season. Serve immediately.

Roasted Pumpkin, Yellow Pepper and Walnut Salad

For this salad you need pumpkin that holds its shape. We always use the big grey-skinned pumpkin called 'Crown'.

SERVES 4–6

500g pumpkin (peeled, de-seeded and cubed)
2 yellow peppers (deseeded and sliced)
olive oil
Maldon sea salt and freshly ground black pepper
100g (1 small) red onion (peeled and finely sliced)
1 celery stalk (chopped)
3 spring onions (chopped)
¼ cup roasted walnuts (roughly chopped)
30ml (2 tblsp) extra virgin olive oil
15ml (1 tblsp) sherry vinegar
handful chervil or Italian parsley (chopped)

+ Preheat oven to 250ºC.
+ Toss pumpkin cubes and pepper strips in olive oil, sprinkle with salt and pepper and lay on a low-sided roasting tray. Roast for about 15 minutes or until pumpkin is fork-tender and peppers are lightly browned.
+ When vegetables are cool enough to handle, combine with onion, celery, spring onions and walnuts.
+ Combine extra virgin olive oil, sherry vinegar and salt and pepper to taste and dress the salad.
+ Sprinkle with chopped herbs and serve on a big platter or in individual bowls.

The Most Tasty Vinaigrette

MAKES 440ml/1¾ CUPS

3 cloves garlic (peeled)
2 tsp dry mustard
1 tblsp mild mustard
½ tsp salt
freshly ground black pepper
2 tsp sugar
¼ cup (60ml) balsamic vinegar
1½ cups (375ml) olive oil

+ Process all ingredients in a food processor fitted with a metal blade.
+ Store in a container in the pantry.

Diane's Kumara and Black Bean Salad

A friend and colleague Diane Kenerdine and I taught a cooking class in Houston several years ago. We served Kumara and Black Bean Salad with barbecued butterflied leg of lamb. This is my version of Diane's salad.

←

Selection of winter salads: Diane's Kumara and Black Bean; Roasted Pumpkin, Yellow Pepper and Walnut; Spinach and Bacon

SERVES 4–6

500g kumara (peeled)[1]
15ml (1 tblsp) salad oil
Maldon sea salt and freshly ground black pepper
30ml (2 tblsp) salad oil
15ml (1 tblsp) Black Bean Garlic Sauce[2]
2 tsp honey (try manuka)
2 tsp lemon juice
6 generous handfuls of salad greens
2 tblsp slivered almonds (toasted)
2 tblsp pumpkin seeds (toasted)
50g mung bean sprouts (or snowpea shoots)
3–5 spring onions (sliced)

+ Preheat oven to 220ºC.
+ Slice kumara on the diagonal, toss with first measure of salad oil and place on a low-sided roasting tray. Season with salt and pepper.
+ Roast kumara for 10–15 minutes or until crispy and golden.
+ To make the dressing whisk second measure of salad oil with Black Bean Garlic Sauce, honey and lemon juice. Season to taste
+ Toss kumara in dressing (flavour improves if dressing is allowed to soak into kumara for about 15 minutes). Arrange salad greens on a platter or in individual bowls, and place kumara on top.
+ Garnish with almonds, pumpkin seeds, sprouts and spring onions.

NOTE: 1. I prefer to use golden kumara for this salad. 2. Black Bean Garlic Sauce is available in supermarkets or Asian supply stores.

Little Pumpkin Gratins

These gratins can be made one or two days ahead and baked when you are ready to serve them.

400g pumpkin (peeled weight)
15g (1 tblsp) butter
30ml (2 tblsp) cream
1 egg yolk
1 tsp chopped parsley
freshly grated nutmeg
Maldon sea salt and freshly
   ground black pepper
melted butter for greasing
   ovenproof ramekins

+ Cut pumpkin into even-sized pieces and steam until soft.
+ Add butter to pumpkin and mash until smooth.
+ Combine cream and egg yolk in a small bowl. Slowly pour into pumpkin mixture and stir.
+ Add parsley, nutmeg and seasoning to taste.
+ Preheat oven to 180°C.
+ Grease 2 ovenproof ramekins with butter. Place pumpkin mixture into prepared ramekins and bake for 20–25 minutes or until pumpkin is hot and slightly puffed up.

Hazelnut Cream Cheese Stuffing

Do not use reduced fat cream cheese or easy spread cream cheese in this recipe unless it is essential. They do not respond as well to mixing or cooking.

30g cream cheese (softened)
1 tsp onion juice[1]
1 tsp lemon juice
dash of brandy
30g (2 tblsp) roasted hazelnuts
   (roughly skinned and
   coarsely chopped)
1 spring onion (finely chopped)
Maldon sea salt and freshly
   ground black pepper

+ Combine cream cheese with onion juice, lemon juice and brandy and stir until smooth.
+ Add remaining ingredients and combine, seasoning to taste.

NOTE: 1. Obtain onion juice on the finest part of your grater, or use a Microplane.

Preserved Lemons

Lift lemons out of the jar with tongs so the bacteria on your hands doesn't contaminate the rest of the jar. Use chopped preserved lemon rind as a flavour enhancer to salads, pasta or fish dishes.

MAKES A 1-LITRE JAR

8 lemons
½ cup salt
1 cinnamon stick
4 bayleaves
freshly squeezed lemon juice
  (as needed)

+   Cut each lemon into quarters from the top to within 5mm of the bottom, leaving the four pieces joined at the stem end. Sprinkle the inside of the lemon with salt.
+   Place 1 tblsp salt on the bottom of a preserving jar and pack the lemons into the jar, pushing them down and adding more salt as you go.
+   Push the cinnamon stick and bayleaves between the lemons.
+   If the level of the lemon juice doesn't come to the top of the jar, add extra freshly squeezed juice to almost the top of the jar. Leave some air space before closing the jar.
+   Let the lemons sit for 1 month, turning the jar upside-down periodically to distribute the salt and juices. Once opened store in the fridge.
+   To use the lemons, remove from the brine and discard the pulp. Wash the peel and use. Some white crystals will form on the top of the lemons in the jar, which is normal so do not discard the lemons.

Bacon-wrapped Turkey Medallions with Hazelnut Cream Cheese Stuffing

Single people or small families do not have the opportunity to cook a whole turkey. Try this dish for a mid-winter Christmas if you are cooking for small numbers. Turkey medallions can be prepared one or two days in advance and stored in the fridge until you are ready to cook them.

→

Bacon-wrapped Turkey Medallions with Hazelnut Cream Cheese Stuffing

SERVES 2

2 turkey tenderloins
    (about 150g)
1 recipe Hazelnut Cream
    Cheese Stuffing
    (see page 62)
2–4 slices of middle bacon
    (rindless) (40–80g)
butter for greasing roasting
    tray

+ Preheat oven to 200°C.
+ Lay tenderloin between plastic wrap or in a plastic bag on a board. Using a meat mallet gently pound tenderloin until it is about half the original thickness.
+ Along the length of tenderloin, lay a thin sausage of Hazelnut Cream Cheese stuffing and roll tenderloin to enclose the stuffing, with seamside down.
+ Wrap 1 to 2 slices of bacon around tenderloin and push 2 wooden toothpicks through tenderloin to secure bacon.
+ Repeat with the second tenderloin.
+ Place tenderloins on a buttered roasting tray and roast for 20–25 minutes or until juices run clear.[1] Remove toothpicks and slice into medallions.

NOTE: 1. If you love roast potatoes add some cubed, peeled potatoes to the turkey tray and roast with the turkey. Toss them in a very small amount of olive oil first. You could also roast other vegetables. Accompany turkey and potatoes with freshly cooked green beans and Little Pumpkin Gratins (see page 62).

Hot Roasted Vegetables

This is a Clayton's version of roasted vegetables. They are low fat and quick cooking. Add some chopped celery, spring onions, parsley and roasted walnut halves to any leftover roasted vegetables. Dress with your favourite dressing and you will have a sensational winter salad. Even cook extra vegetables so you can make this salad.

SERVES 2

400g vegetables,[1] choose a combination of yams, parsnips, Jerusalem artichokes, pumpkin, kumara, turnips, swedes, beetroot, leeks, peppers, mushrooms, zucchinis or potatoes.

olive oil

Maldon sea salt and freshly ground black pepper

chopped herbs of your choice (parsley, sage, thyme, winter savory)

+ Preheat oven to 220°C.
+ Peel the vegetables you would prefer peeled and cut all into 1cm cubes.
+ Toss prepared vegetables with olive oil[2] so oil just coats them.
+ Season vegetables and place on low-sided[3] roasting tray (a sponge roll tin will do). Do not overcrowd your roasting tray.
+ Place tray in oven and cook vegetables for around 15 minutes until they are soft and browned.
+ When vegetables are cooked, sprinkle with chopped herbs and add further seasoning if you wish.

NOTE: 1. If you are cooking for one look in your supermarket for pre-prepared packets of vegetables. 2. Using an oil spray pump, seen in many kitchen shops, you can quickly spray vegetables with oil. 3. The low sides are important if you are hot roasting.

Creamed Spinach

Leftover Creamed Spinach is delicious served on Vogel's toast with crispy bacon, grilled cheese or even a poached egg. Make this recipe in advance and reheat as you need it in the microwave. You can thin down leftover Creamed Spinach with milk, water or chicken stock and serve as soup.

SERVES 4

60g butter
1 tblsp finely chopped onion
1 clove garlic
   (peeled and finely chopped)
30g flour
200ml milk
200ml cream
1 cup cooked spinach[1]
   (squeezed dry and finely
   chopped)
Maldon sea salt and freshly
   ground black pepper
freshly grated nutmeg

+ In a heavy-based pot, melt butter and cook onion and garlic until soft and transparent. Stir in flour to make a roux and cook for 2–3 minutes (without colouring).
+ Slowly add milk and cream (stirring constantly) to make a thick sauce.
+ Bring sauce to the boil and simmer for 5 minutes.
+ Stir in spinach and heat through.
+ Season Creamed Spinach with salt, pepper and nutmeg.

NOTE: 1. We use Wattie's Frozen Spinach which comes cooked in 250g boxes. One box is enough spinach to make one recipe.

Bacon-wrapped Fillet of Beef with Hot Roasted Vegetables and Creamed Spinach

I often meet people who live alone and don't bother to spoil themselves. This is a luxurious little dinner for someone who lives alone. Leftover cooked beef fillet will keep, covered, in the fridge for 2–3 days. Have it cold for lunch with a salad or make delicious Vogel's bread sandwiches with lettuce, tomato and horseradish cream.

→
Bacon-wrapped Fillet of Beef with Hot Roasted Vegetables and Creamed Spinach

SERVES 2

400g beef fillet
    (trimmed weight)
2 slices bacon
handful of herbs (rosemary,
    oregano or thyme)
olive oil
freshly ground black pepper
Hot Roasted Vegetables
    (see page 66)
Creamed Spinach
    (see page 67)

+ Ask your butcher to trim the silverskin from the beef fillet.
+ Preheat oven to 220°C.
+ Wrap bacon around beef fillet.
+ Place beef in a low-sided roasting tray (a sponge roll tin will do) on a bed of fresh herbs. Smear with olive oil and sprinkle with pepper.
+ Roast beef for 15 minutes or until just medium rare. Remove from oven and cover roasting tray with a heavy teatowel. Rest beef for 10 minutes (this allows the muscles to relax and the juices to disperse throughout the meat).
+ When ready to serve, carve beef fillet and place 2–3 slices on your most beautiful plate. Serve with wholegrain mustard.

Orzo and Vegetable Salad

Orzo is a rice-shaped pasta. Combine the salad while the orzo is hot or warm.

SERVES 6–8

75g (½ cup) snowpeas (blanched 20 seconds in boiling water)

50g (½) red onion (finely sliced)

100g (½ cup) cherry tomatoes (halved)

½ red and ½ yellow pepper (deseeded, roasted and peeled)

200g (1 cup) orzo cooked until al dente (drained)

2 tsp preserved lemon rind[1] (finely chopped)

¼ cup extra virgin olive oil

2 tsp liquid from preserved lemons

freshly ground black pepper

a large handful baby rocket leaves

+ Put snowpeas, onion, tomatoes and peppers into a bowl and combine with orzo.
+ Just before serving toss preserved lemon rind through. Mix oil with liquid from preserved lemons and pepper to make a dressing, seasoning with black pepper.
+ Dress salad. Sprinkle salad with rocket leaves.

NOTE: 1. Preserved lemon rind really enhances this salad (see page 63).

Chicken Breasts with Pesto, Mozzarella and Sun-dried Tomatoes

Serve this chicken dish with potatoes baked in their jackets, or better still with garlic mashed potatoes and some green beans.

SERVES 2

1½ tblsp olive oil (or oil from sun-dried tomatoes)
1 small clove garlic (peeled and finely chopped)
½ tblsp soy sauce
freshly ground black pepper
2 chicken breasts (skin off)
15g (1 tblsp) Basil Pesto (below)
15g (1 tblsp) sun-dried tomatoes (drained and chopped)
50g mozzarella[1] (sliced)
30g (3 tblsp) Parmesan (grated)
Maldon sea salt, freshly ground black pepper and lemon juice

+ Mix olive oil, garlic, soy sauce, a grind of pepper and toss chicken in this mixture.
+ Marinate chicken for 15–30 minutes.
+ Preheat oven to 220°C. Drain chicken of excess marinade, discard marinade, and place chicken in a low-sided roasting tray. Bake for 7–8 minutes or until chicken is three-quarters cooked.
+ Remove chicken from oven and spread top of chicken with pesto, sprinkle with sun-dried tomatoes and place mozzarella on top. Sprinkle Parmesan over chicken and cook for a further 5–6 minutes or until mozzarella is melted and golden brown, and chicken juices run clear.
+ Season with lemon juice, salt and pepper.

NOTE: 1. Mozzarella is a fresh cheese with a delicate milky flavour.

Basil Pesto

MAKES 120G

1 clove garlic (peeled)
50g (⅓ cup) pine nuts
45g (½ cup) basil leaves
45g (⅓ cup) grated Parmesan
50ml (¼ cup) olive oil
Maldon sea salt and freshly ground black pepper
lemon juice to taste

+ Put garlic, pine nuts, basil and Parmesan into food processor fitted with metal blade. Process until smooth.
+ Pour in olive oil through feed tube with processor going slowly
+ Add salt, pepper and lemon juice to taste.

Moroccan Spiced Chicken with Orzo and Vegetable Salad

←

Moroccan Spiced Chicken with Orzo and Vegetable Salad

The carrot juice in the marinade makes the chicken very sweet, tender and juicy. Chicken thigh as opposed to chicken breast is a more reliable cut in terms of producing a juicy result.

SERVES 8

60ml (¼ cup) olive oil
125ml (½ cup) carrot juice[1]
grated zest of 1 lemon
handful coriander (chopped)
1.6kg boneless chicken thighs
   (skin on)
1 tblsp ground cumin
1 tblsp smoked paprika
1 tblsp Maldon sea salt
Orzo and Vegetable Salad
   (see page 70)

+ In a non-reactive bowl, combine olive oil, carrot juice, lemon zest and coriander.
+ Add chicken and toss to coat. Cover and refrigerate for at least 2–3 hours or overnight.
+ Preheat barbecue.[2]
+ Remove chicken from marinade and pat dry with paper towels. Discard marinade.
+ In a small bowl, combine cumin, smoked paprika and salt. Season thighs generously with this mixture.
+ Place chicken skin side down onto barbecue and cook for 5–6 minutes each side or until juices run clear.
+ Once cooked, transfer chicken to a roasting tray and cover with tin foil. Allow to rest for 10 minutes before serving.

NOTE: 1. You need to juice approximately 200g topped and tailed carrots to make 125ml of juice. You may find it ready-made perhaps at a supermarket, but more likely at an organic produce shop. 2. Alternatively, preheat oven to 200°C. Place chicken skin side down on a low-sided roasting tray, allowing 2cm between each piece. Roast, uncovered, for 15–18 minutes or until juices run clear.

Fillet Steak with Béarnaise Sauce, Chips and Rocket

←

Fillet Steak with Béarnaise Sauce, Chips and Rocket

You are not worth your salt as a chef unless you can cook a mean steak. Buy the best beef possible, open a window and place a cast-iron frying pan on a high heat until it smokes. Smear the pan with olive oil and begin. Sear the steak on each side initially, and then cook on each side. Don't play with it while it cooks.

SERVES 4

600–800g beef fillet
  (trimmed weight)
olive oil for smearing the pan
Béarnaise Sauce (see page 76)
Chips
4 generous handfuls of young
  rocket[1]
Maldon sea salt and freshly
  ground black pepper

+ Cut beef into 4 steaks and cook to your liking. As it cooks do not prod and poke it as you will push the juice out of the steak.
+ Rest steaks on a warmed plate covered with a heavy teatowel for at least five minutes after cooking. This will allow the juices to distribute through the steak.
+ Place a steak on a warmed dinner plate, drizzle with Béarnaise Sauce, accompany with Chips and scatter rocket over the dish. Season with lots of salt and a little pepper.

NOTE: 1. Rocket: For really good rocket grow your own. Plant it in the garden, terracotta pot, a tub or even a hanging basket. You can grow it from seeds, but water very frequently. It loves water. Treat it gently and eat it young.

Chips

These are great low fat, no mess chips.

SERVES 4–6

400–800g peeled potatoes
  (preferably Agria)
olive oil
Maldon sea salt and freshly
  ground black pepper

+ Preheat oven to 220°C.
+ Cut potatoes into wedges lengthways.
+ Spray a low-sided baking tray with olive oil and arrange potato wedges in a single layer on tray. Place the potato wedges so that they don't touch.
+ Spray potatoes with olive oil and season with salt and pepper.
+ Place in oven and hot roast without turning for 25–30 minutes or until golden brown.

NOTE: I keep some olive oil in a Misto in my kitchen. A Misto is a vaporiser spray bottle.

Béarnaise Sauce

This can be made in the food processor, but if you make it in a bowl over a pot of simmering water using a whisk you will achieve a thicker, more unctuous result. Guests are always impressed by a host who has the confidence to make a hand-whisked Béarnaise Sauce in front of them, particularly if you are able to hold a conversation in the process. The secret to this sort of confidence is preparation beforehand – have everything measured, and your equipment at the ready.

Grow French (not Russian) tarragon close to your house, or in a pot on the deck or windowsill, and keep it for Béarnaise Sauce, for chook stuffing, or adding to scrambled eggs.

SERVES 4–6

3 tblsp tarragon vinegar
150g unsalted butter (diced)
3 egg yolks
3 tblsp water
3 tblsp chopped fresh tarragon
Maldon sea salt and freshly
   ground black pepper

+ Put vinegar into a tiny pot and reduce by half. In another pot melt butter and cool to lukewarm.
+ Put reduced vinegar, egg yolks and water in a bowl and place over a pot of simmering water.[1]
+ Whisk the mixture in the bowl until it becomes fluffy and light. (Keep the water underneath the bowl simmering only – not boiling).
+ When the egg yolk mixture and melted butter are of a similar temperature (lukewarm), slowly pour the melted butter, drop by drop, into the egg yolk mixture, whisking all the time. (If the water underneath, or the mixture you are whisking, gets above lukewarm temperature, remove from heat).
+ When you have used up all the butter, your sauce will be thick and silky.
+ Add tarragon and season with salt and pepper.

NOTE: 1. Alternative method is to combine vinegar, egg yolks and water in a food processor and slowly pour melted butter through feed tube with the processor running.

Pork Chops à la Celine

My friend Celine serves this dish with Pommes de Terre à la Boulangère and carrots cooked with butter and parsley. She also prepares steamed broccoli with a well-made white sauce (see page 86). Celine's pork chops are delicious eaten cold with salad, little gherkins and mustard.

SERVES 8

handful of fresh thyme
2–2.5 kg pork rack with 9 ribs,
   rind on
Maldon sea salt and freshly
   ground black pepper
20 cloves garlic
   (peeled and chopped)
10–15 fresh bayleaves

+ Preheat oven to 150ºC.
+ Strip thyme leaves and discard stalks.
+ Cut pork rack into cutlets and coat cutlets all over with salt, pepper, thyme and garlic.
+ Cut a piece of aluminium foil to about the size of a big newspaper page and place a double row of bayleaves down the centre of the foil.
+ Re-form cutlets back into a rack and place onto the bayleaves.
+ Wrap foil like you would fish and chips. Add more layers of foil until pork is wrapped in 4 layers.
+ Place parcel in roasting tray and bake for 3 hours.
+ Let parcel rest for 15 minutes, unwrap and serve.

Pommes de Terre à la Boulangère

Serve with Pork Chops à la Celine. These potatoes are traditionally cooked round a joint of meat baked in the oven.

SERVES 8

small handful of thyme
900g[1] (18 med) potatoes,
   peeled and cubed
150g (1 large) onion, peeled
   and chopped
Maldon sea salt and freshly
   ground black pepper
125ml (½ cup) stock
   (beef or chicken)
60g (½ cup) butter (cubed)
2 fresh bayleaves

+ Preheat oven to 150ºC.
+ Strip thyme leaves and discard stalks.
+ Place all ingredients into a deep roasting tray and mix ingredients together with your hands.
+ Cover roasting tray tightly with aluminium foil and bake for 1 hour or until potatoes are soft.

NOTE: 1. Celine always portions 2 potatoes per guest and 2 for the pot. She prefers to use Desirèe potatoes for this dish.

Whole Hot Roasted Salmon with Jersey Benne Potatoes

←

Whole Hot Roasted Salmon with Jersey Benne Potatoes

Order your whole salmon ahead from your supermarket or fish shop. Judge a salmon for freshness as you would fish, the eyes should be clear and there should be absolutely no odour. I love this dish either hot, room temperature or cold, and any leftovers are great in a salad – or wonderful for salmon pie or salmon cakes.

At the table carve the salmon with a dessert slice and knife, using scissors to cut pieces of crispy skin for your guests. When you have carved one side flip the salmon over, or alternatively pull the vertebrae to one side to allow you to carve the second side.

SERVES 10

3kg whole salmon
  (scaled and gutted)
45ml (3 tblsp) olive oil
  (plus extra for potatoes)
45ml (3 tblsp) lemon juice
3 tblsp Maldon sea salt
freshly ground black pepper
1.5kg Jersey Benne potatoes
  (washed, dried and tossed
  in olive oil)

+ Position oven rack in centre of the oven. Preheat oven to 250ºC.
+ Wash and dry salmon. With a large sharp knife, cut 3 diagonal slashes into each side of fish, cutting in nearly to bone.
+ Just before salmon goes into the oven combine olive oil, lemon juice, salt and pepper and rub all over salmon, including in the slashes and the cavity.
+ Put salmon on diagonal in a low-sided tray[1] (don't worry if head or tail hang over the side!).
+ Add prepared potatoes to tray and roast salmon and potatoes for 32 minutes (a 2kg salmon will take 27 minutes).
+ Remove tray from oven and using 2 fish slices and a friend, transfer salmon to a serving platter. Transfer potatoes to salmon platter, or to a separate bowl.

NOTE: 1. The secret of success to hot roasting is the roasting tray you cook on. You require a low-sided tray so that the heat from the oven can transfer easily to the item in the tray.

Salmon with Honey Mustard Dressing

Salmon stays very moist when you cook it with the skin on.

→
Ladle of Honey Mustard Dressing

SERVES 4

4 x 150g pieces fresh salmon
 (bone out and skin on)
1 recipe Salmon Marinade
olive oil
1 recipe Honey Mustard
 Dressing (below)

SALMON MARINADE

½ cup olive oil
1 garlic clove (finely chopped)
1 tblsp soy sauce

+ Place salmon into a non-reactive dish with marinade[1] and leave for a minimum of 20 minutes or up to 1 hour.
+ Preheat oven to 220°C.
+ Spray or brush a low-sided baking tray with olive oil. Remove salmon from marinade and place skin side down on the tray.
+ Bake in oven for 6–8 minutes or until salmon is cooked medium rare.
+ Serve with Honey Mustard Dressing and asparagus.
+ To make marinade, combine oil, soy sauce and garlic in a small bowl.

NOTES: 1. For each salmon dish we make we always marinate it first in this marinade.

Honey Mustard Dressing

I first enjoyed this dressing with salmon prepared by Michael Lee-Richards as part of a Perfect Pinot Paring session.

1 clove garlic (finely chopped)
1 tblsp finely chopped red onion
½ tsp mustard powder
2 tblsp liquid honey
1 tsp lemon zest
4 tblsp lemon juice
4 tblsp olive oil
Maldon sea salt and freshly
 ground black pepper
2 tblsp currants
2 medium tomatoes (blanched,
 peeled, deseeded and
 chopped)
2 tblsp finely chopped Italian
 parsley

+ Combine the first 8 ingredients in a bowl and whisk to blend.
+ Add currants and set aside to allow currants to plump up. Before serving, stir in tomato and parsley.

Hot Roasted Fish with Ginger, Soy and Coriander

My favourite fish for this dish is Chatham Island blue cod, but any firm, fresh fish is absolutely fine. The secret to this recipe is the cooking method – 'hot roasting'. You will need a low-sided baking tray so the intensity of your oven can quickly transfer to the fish. There is something you may need to convince your fishmonger of – most fish dishes, and especially this one, are so much juicier if the fish has the skin on. This dish works equally well with salmon.

↑

Hot Roasted Fish with Ginger, Soy and Coriander served with Coconut Rice Timbale

SERVES 4 AS A MAIN COURSE

600–800g fish fillet
   (firm, fresh fish with skin
   on and bone out)
1 recipe Ginger, Soy and
   Coriander Marinade
   (opposite)
Maldon sea salt
coriander leaves and lime
   halves to garnish

+ Preheat oven to 250°C.
+ Cut fillets into 150–200g portions, leaving skin on.
+ Coat fish in some of the marinade mixture and leave for up to 1 hour. (Freeze remainder of marinade.)
+ Remove fish from marinade and place skin side up on a low-sided baking tray.
+ Depending on the thickness of the fish, roast for 5–10 minutes, or until it is just cooked.
+ Sprinkle with salt and garnish with coriander and lime halves. Serve with Coconut Rice Timbales (opposite).

Coconut Rice Timbales

Prepare these ahead if you wish and reheat in dariole moulds for service.

SERVES 4–6

approx. 12 threads saffron
250ml (1 cup) chicken stock
15g (1 tblsp) butter
20g shallots (1 shallot) (peeled
    and finely chopped)
1 clove garlic (peeled and
    finely chopped)
3cm piece peeled ginger root
    (grated)
½ red chilli (deseeded and
    finely chopped)
210g (1 cup) jasmine rice
250ml (1 cup) coconut cream
juice of 3 small limes and
    zest of 2
Maldon sea salt and freshly
    ground black pepper
handful fresh coriander leaves
    (finely chopped)

+ Preheat oven to 180°C. Sauté saffron in dry frying pan over moderate heat for 2–3 minutes.
+ Bring stock to the boil and add saffron. Remove from heat and set aside.
+ Melt butter in small ovenproof pot, add shallots, garlic and ginger. Soften for a few minutes without colouring. Add chilli and keep cooking for a minute or two. Stir in rice and sauté for 1–2 minutes without colouring.
+ Reheat stock. Pour hot stock, coconut cream and lime juice into rice mixture and add lime zest. Stir and bring to the boil. Add seasoning.
+ Cover rice with tinfoil (pushing it down to the level of the rice and up the sides of the pot) and cover pot with a tight-fitting lid.
+ Bake for 15–17 minutes or until rice is soft to the bite. Fluff up rice and add coriander. Taste for seasoning and cool.
+ Mould rice into ungreased dariole moulds, reheat (covered) in roasting tray half filled with water for 30–40 minutes at 160°C. Unmould and serve.

Ginger, Soy and Coriander Marinade

60ml (¼ cup) sesame oil
60ml (¼ cup) soy sauce
3cm peeled ginger root (grated)
2 stalks lemongrass (thicker
    bulb part finely chopped)
bunch of coriander (leaves,
    stems and roots chopped)

+ Combine all ingredients.

Old-fashioned Salmon Pie

This is a great do-ahead dish for supper or weekend lunches. You can also make it in individual ramekins. Serve it with a salad or, if you are feeling homely, a big bowl of minted, buttered green peas and Week Night Rainbow Chard (see page 86).

→
Old-fashioned Salmon Pie

**SERVES 12 AS PART OF A
BUFFET OR 8 AS A SINGLE
MAIN COURSE**

1kg salmon
   (boned and cooked)[1]
8 eggs (hardboiled)
White Sauce (see page 86)
Mashed Potato (below)
100g tasty cheese (grated)
50g Italian Parmesan (grated)

+ Flake salmon into the base of a greased 2.5 litre ovenproof gratin dish.
+ Peel eggs and slice in half lengthways. Place eggs cut side down onto salmon.
+ Pour sauce over eggs and salmon and allow sauce to cool slightly.
+ Spread mashed potato on top of sauce and smooth out with a spatula. Sprinkle with the two cheeses (you can refrigerate pie at this stage).
+ Preheat oven to 180°C.
+ Bake for 35–45 minutes or until pie is hot through and potato is golden brown.

NOTE: 1. If at any time you have leftover salmon, cook and freeze so you can make this pie later. Cook the salmon by grilling or hot roasting (220°C for 5–10 minutes).

Mashed Potato
(for Old-fashioned Salmon Pie)

The egg yolk in this mashed potato gives lightness to the potatoes when they are reheated.

1.5kg potato
   (peeled and chopped)
50g butter (diced)
60ml (4 tblsp) cream
1 egg yolk
freshly grated nutmeg
Maldon sea salt and white
   pepper

+ Steam potatoes until tender.
+ Place potatoes in a bowl and mash. Add remaining ingredients and beat together until smooth and fluffy.

Week Night Rainbow Chard

Rainbow Chard looks so vibrant in the flower or vege garden that it hurts to pick it.

SERVES 4

500–750g Rainbow Chard with
    stalks (washed and roughly
    diced)
2 tblsp water
1 tblsp olive oil
1 tblsp butter
Maldon sea salt and freshly
    ground black pepper

+   Place all ingredients in a large pot and simmer
    for 5 minutes or until wilted.

White Sauce
(for Old-fashioned Salmon Pie)

I believe this is one of the most difficult sauces to make well. Sufficient cooking
of the roux and the gradual addition of liquid makes a good white sauce.

750ml (3 cups) cream
750ml (3 cups) milk
70g butter
40g (4 small) shallots
    (peeled and finely chopped)
3 cloves garlic
    (peeled and finely chopped)
70g (½ cup) flour
5 spring onions (chopped)
bunch Italian parsley or chervil
    (chopped)
Maldon sea salt and freshly
    ground black pepper
freshly ground nutmeg

+   Pour cream and milk into a pot and heat to just
    below boiling point.
+   Over a moderate heat, melt butter in a heavy-
    bottomed saucepan, add shallots and garlic and
    sauté (without browning) until soft and transparent.
+   Add flour all at once and stir to make a roux.[1]
+   Remove roux from the heat and cool slightly.
    Gradually pour on hot cream and milk, stirring each
    pour until it has amalgamated with the roux before
    you add the next pour.
+   Once cream and milk have been added, bring sauce
    to the boil and simmer for approximately 20 minutes.
    Add spring onions and parsley and season to taste
    with salt, pepper and nutmeg.

NOTE: 1. Cook out the flour for 2–3 minutes stirring occasionally
to prevent it from sticking.

Avocado, Orange and Mint Salad

Serve this salad as an accompaniment to Whole Hot Roasted Salmon with Jersey Benne Potatoes (see page 79). Segment the oranges the day before, but leave the preparation of the avocados until you are ready to serve the salad. If you think segmenting the oranges is too much trouble, then cut the oranges into rounds.

SERVES 8

4 avocados
4 oranges (pink grapefruit or
    mandarins are also delicious)
6–10 spring onions
    (the smaller the better)
big handful mint sprigs
Orange Dressing (below)

+ Halve, peel, stone and slice avocados into chunky slices.
+ Peel oranges, removing skin and pith, and segment. Alternate avocado and orange on a platter.
+ Trim spring onions, leave whole if they are small or, if large, cut on diagonal. Scatter spring onions and mint sprigs over avocado and orange, and drizzle with Orange Dressing.

Orange Dressing

MAKES 105ML

60ml (¼ cup) extra virgin olive oil
15ml (1 tblsp) balsamic
    vinegar
1 tsp finely grated orange zest
½ tsp Maldon sea salt
grind of pepper
30ml (2 tblsp) fresh orange juice
    (save juice from segmented
    oranges)

+ Whisk all ingredients together in a bowl.

Roast Leg of Lamb with Oranges, Red Onions and Mint

Serve lamb hot or warm with Yams with Balsamic Vinegar (opposite) or kumaras baked in their jackets. Green beans go well with this dish.

←

Roast Leg of Lamb with Oranges, Red Onions and Mint

SERVES 6–8

500g (2 medium) red onions (peeled and thinly sliced)
2 oranges (thinly sliced into rounds with skin on)
1.5–2kg leg of lamb (at room temperature)
45ml (3 tblsp) olive oil
45ml (3 tblsp) freshly squeezed orange juice
1 handful mint (chopped)
Maldon sea salt and freshly ground black pepper
250ml (1 cup) freshly squeezed orange juice
mint sprigs

+ Preheat oven to 250ºC.
+ Place onion In a roasting pan and top with ½ of the orange slices. Place lamb on top of onion and orange.
+ Mix olive oil and first measure of orange juice and brush over lamb and sprinkle with mint, salt and pepper. Place remaining orange slices on lamb.
+ Roast lamb for 10 minutes and then reduce heat to 220ºC. Roast lamb for a further 45–50 minutes or until it is cooked medium rare.
+ Remove lamb from roasting pan and rest covered[1] for at least 15 minutes but ideally for 30 minutes. With a slotted spoon remove onions and oranges to a serving platter. Put the roasting pan with meat juices onto a high heat on stove-top and add second measure of orange juice. Season to taste.[2]
+ Carve lamb and place on serving platter. Drizzle with a little sauce and garnish with mint sprigs. Serve a jug of sauce separately.

NOTE: 1. For red meat, rest covered with a clean towel (or several teatowels) as opposed to aluminium foil. 2. A dash of balsamic vinegar can make the sauce even more delicious.

Yams with Balsamic Vinegar

Potatoes or pumpkin are also delicious roasted with balsamic vinegar. These yams go brilliantly with Roast Leg of Lamb with Oranges, Red Onions and Mint.

SERVES 6–8

600–800g yams
45ml (3 tblsp) olive oil
45ml (3 tblsp) balsamic vinegar
handful chopped thyme leaves
Maldon sea salt and freshly ground black pepper

+ Preheat oven to 220°C.
+ Toss ingredients together and place on a low-sided roasting tray and roast for 15–20 minutes or until the yams are golden and soft centred.

Kiwiana Salad

Like a Salad Niçoise from France, this salad was probably invented in England to use up bits and pieces. The thrifty housewife picked produce from her small garden and eeked it out with home preserves. I love this salad with pickled beetroot, fresh asparagus and pullets' eggs. (If you can't buy pullets' eggs at your supermarket, insist because egg farms nearly always have them and have difficulty getting supermarkets to buy them. They are the small and perfectly formed eggs from the new laying young hens! Just the right size for this salad). Serve with barbecued butterfly lamb leg.

→
Kiwiana Salad

SERVES 10

5 pullet eggs

30 asparagus spears (ends pinged and discarded)

iceberg lettuce (3–4 iceberg hearts only if you are extravagant)

½ cucumber (peeled and cut into 5mm-thick slices on the diagonal)

20 baby spring onions (trimmed)

20 small radishes (washed, trimmed and halved)

20 baby pickled beetroot (cut into quarters)

10 small gherkins

1 cup grated tasty or colby cheese

1 recipe Salad Cream (opposite)

3 egg whites (cooked)[1]

Maldon sea salt and freshly ground black pepper

+ Place eggs in a pot and cover with cold water. Bring pot to the boil and boil eggs for 5 minutes exactly. Refresh eggs immediately under cold running water, then peel and cut into halves. This will give you firm whites and slightly runny yolks.

+ Bring a medium-sized pot of water to the boil. Add asparagus and blanch for 1–2 minutes or until bright green and al dente. Refresh immediately under cold water. Drain well.

+ Separate lettuce hearts (or lettuce) into leaves and arrange on a big platter. Place cucumber, asparagus, spring onions, radishes and eggs on top of the lettuce and season with salt and pepper.

+ Place beetroot, gherkins and cheese into separate small bowls.

+ Drizzle Salad Cream over the salad and garnish with chopped egg whites.

NOTE: 1. These are the egg whites from the hard-boiled eggs cooked for the Salad Cream.

Salad Cream

This Salad Cream is also delicious with new season's Bluff oysters served 'natural', or as the dressing for warm Jersey Benne potatoes.

MAKES 225ML

3 eggs (hard-boiled)
1 tsp sugar
1 tsp dry English mustard
   powder
1 tblsp tarragon vinegar
1 tblsp chopped fresh tarragon
140ml cream
Maldon sea salt and freshly
   ground black pepper

+ Separate cooked egg whites and egg yolks. Reserve egg whites for use in the salad.
+ Whisk yolks, sugar, mustard and vinegar together.
+ Add tarragon and cream and whisk until slightly thickened. Season to taste.

Roast Peppered Ribeye of Beef with Au Jus, Yorkshire Puddings and Horseradish Cream

←

Roast Peppered Ribeye of Beef with Au Jus, Yorkshire Puddings and Horseradish Cream

The following method will give you juicy, tasty beef. Carve in front of your guests and watch them come back to secretly nibble on the bones.

SERVES 8

2–3kg ribeye of beef (bone in)[1]
2 tblsp Dijon mustard
4 tblsp black peppercorns
   (crushed in a mortar and
   pestle)
1 tblsp Maldon sea salt
250ml (1 cup) red wine
250ml (1 cup) beef stock
Horseradish Cream
   (see page 94)

+ Remove beef from refrigerator for at least 1 hour before cooking to bring it to room temperature. Remove silverskin[2] from beef.
+ Preheat oven to 250°C.
+ Brush beef with mustard and roll in peppercorns and salt to coat evenly.
+ Place beef in roasting tray, bone side down and roast for 45 minutes.
+ Reduce heat to 200°C and roast for a further 25–30 minutes.
+ Remove beef from oven and transfer to a warmed serving platter. Cover with thick teatowels and allow beef to rest[3] for at least 15 minutes.
+ To make Au Jus pour excess fat out of roasting tray and place tray over a high heat. Deglaze[4] tray with red wine and add beef stock. Reduce by half and taste for seasoning.[5]
+ Serve with Yorkshire Puddings (see page 94) and Horseradish Cream.

NOTE: 1. Ask your butcher for bone in ribeye, oven prepared. 2. The silverskin is the silver membrane on meat that shrinks during cooking and if you don't remove it, it distorts the shape of the meat. Silverskin is very tough and chewy to eat. 3. It is important to 'rest' meat after roasting as it allows the juices to solidify and the structure to relax prior to carving. 4. To deglaze a roasting tray is to incorporate all the tasty flavours and sediments from the bottom of the tray with wine. 5. A dash of balsamic vinegar or Worcestershire sauce can zap up your sauce.

MAIN EVENT **93**

Yorkshire Puddings

We sometimes make Yorkshire Puddings ahead and freeze them. Of course, warm them before you serve.

MAKES 8 REGULAR-SIZED MUFFIN TIN PUDDINGS

105g (¾ cup) flour
pinch salt
2 eggs
250ml (1 cup) milk
clarified butter

+ Sieve flour and salt into a medium-sized bowl. Add eggs and milk and beat until smooth.
+ Rest mixture in the fridge for 1 hour.
+ Preheat oven to 220°C.
+ Spray muffin tins with baking spray, and also into each muffin tin put ¼ tsp clarified butter.[1]
+ Place muffin tins in oven for 10–15 minutes until the butter is sizzling.
+ Beat mixture well and pour into muffin tins until 1mm full from the top.
+ Bake for 20–25 minutes until double in size and a rich golden brown colour. Tip out onto a cooling rack and serve immediately or freeze when cool for future use.

NOTE: 1. Traditionally fat from the beef roasting pan is used but we use clarified butter as many people today don't like the taste of beef fat.

Horseradish Cream

MAKES 400ML

300ml cream
1 tblsp fresh horseradish
   (peeled and grated)
2 tblsp prepared horseradish
   sauce
Maldon sea salt and freshly
   ground black pepper

+ Whip cream.
+ Fold horseradish and horseradish sauce into cream and season with salt and pepper.

Beef Fillet Wrapped in Rainbow Chard with Roasted Beetroot Sauce and Oven-roasted Tomatoes

Serve this dish with a full-bodied Cabernet, plain boiled potatoes and green beans. It is a very special dish – the colours are amazing.

SERVES 8–10

1 (1.5–2kg) beef fillet
30ml (2 tblsp) olive oil
1 recipe Horseradish Butter (see page 97)
12–15 (300–400g) rainbow chard leaves[1]
1 recipe Roasted Beetroot Sauce (see page 97)
1 recipe Oven-roasted Tomatoes (see page 97)

+ Trim beef of silverskin and fat. Cut off tail and reserve for a further use.
+ Heat olive oil in a large heavy frying pan, sear beef fillet on all sides and cool. Spread Horseradish Butter all over beef.
+ Cook rainbow chard in boiling water until wilted and refresh in iced water. Place on absorbent paper and blot to remove excess water.
+ Lay out a sheet of plastic wrap (to measure about 35cm by 60cm)[2] and spread out chard (with the underside of chard facing up) to totally cover plastic wrap.
+ Place beef on the chard the side closest to you. Using plastic wrap like you would a sushi mat, roll up beef and chard tightly (make sure you fold the chard in at the ends). Discard plastic wrap, wrap beef tightly in tinfoil and chill for at least 30 minutes or overnight.
+ Preheat oven to 180°C.
+ Place beef on a low-sided bun tray and roast in oven for 25–30 minutes. Remove from oven, leave in tinfoil and rest covered with a heavy teatowel for 15 minutes.
+ To serve: unwrap, slice beef and serve with Roasted Beetroot Sauce and Oven-roasted Tomatoes.

NOTE: 1. Rainbow chard is like silverbeet but with coloured stalks. For this recipe remove the thickest part of the stalk. 2. We use a commercial roll of plastic wrap.

Oven-roasted Tomatoes

SERVES 8

handful of winter savory
45ml (3 tblsp) olive oil
½ tblsp Maldon sea salt
500g (8 medium round)
    tomatoes

+ Preheat oven to 180ºC. Smash savory with oil and salt in a mortar and pestle.
+ Put a cross on bottom end of tomatoes and coat tomatoes in oil mixture. Spread remainder of oil mixture on the bottom of a roasting tray.
+ Place tomatoes in roasting tray, bottom side up.
+ Bake for 30 minutes or until tomatoes are soft.

Horseradish Butter

YIELDS 125G

125g butter
    (diced and softened)
2 tblsp freshly grated
    horseradish[1]
Maldon sea salt and freshly
    ground black pepper

+ Place butter and horseradish into a food processor and process until smooth.
+ Season and taste.

NOTE: 1. You can use prepared horseradish if you wish.

Roasted Beetroot Sauce

This sauce is also great to serve as a dip.

MAKES 750ML

800g beetroot
    (washed and trimmed)
45ml (3 tblsp) olive oil
30ml (2 tblsp) balsamic
    vinegar
250ml (1 cup) unsweetened
    natural yoghurt
Maldon sea salt and freshly
    ground black pepper

+ Preheat oven to 200ºC.
+ Place beetroot in a roasting tray, sprinkle with oil, cover tightly with foil and place in oven.
+ Roast for 1 hour or until tender. Retain any cooking juices.
+ When cool enough to handle, peel, and place into a food processor and purée.
+ Add cooking juices, balsamic vinegar, yoghurt and season to taste.

Forest Mushroom Sauce

MAKES 400ML

15g (½ cup) dried mushrooms
   (French or Italian)
250ml (1 cup) hot water
15g (1 tblsp) duck fat (or olive oil)
50g (½ small) onion (finely
   chopped)
60g mushrooms (sliced)
1 medium carrot
   (peeled and finely chopped)
1 stalk celery (finely chopped)
1 leek (finely chopped)
3 thyme sprigs
1 bayleaf
3 parsley sprigs
2 sage leaves
1 clove garlic (chopped)
1L (4 cups) duck or chicken stock
Maldon sea salt and freshly
   ground black pepper

+ Place dried mushrooms into a bowl and cover with hot water. Set aside to rehydrate.
+ In a saucepan, heat duck fat (or olive oil) over a medium heat, add all the remaining ingredients (except duck stock) and cook until soft.
+ Line a sieve with muslin or a paper towel.[1] Strain water from dried mushrooms and add to saucepan of vegetables with duck or chicken stock.
+ Bring sauce to the boil and simmer until reduced by half. Strain sauce, discard vegetables and add rehydrated mushrooms. Simmer for 5 minutes and season to taste.

NOTE: 1. The mushroom water will be gritty.

Potato Cakes

Make these Potato Cakes a day or two ahead and reheat while you cook and rest the duck.

1.5kg large potatoes[1] (peeled)
75g (3 rashers) bacon
   (finely chopped)
50g (¼ cup) duck fat (or extra
   virgin olive oil)
1 thyme sprig (finely chopped)
Maldon sea salt and freshly
   ground black pepper

NOTE: 1. Preferably Agria. 2. Bake potato cakes while the duck is resting.

+ Steam potatoes until tender and then mash.
+ Cook bacon in a frying pan until lightly coloured.
+ Brush the bottom of 8 individual pie dishes with duck fat (or extra virgin olive oil).
+ Add bacon and thyme to mashed potato with any remaining duck fat (or extra virgin olive oil). Add enough duck fat or extra virgin olive oil so that the mixture is smooth and unctuous. Season with salt and pepper.
+ Fill pie dishes with potato mixture and smooth top.
+ At point of service preheat oven to 200°C.
+ Bake potato cakes in oven for 15–20 minutes or until hot.[2] Invert and serve.

Steak and Kidney Pie

This is a very male friendly main course. Definitely serve with mashed potatoes. If you like oysters slip some raw oysters into the pie just before you serve.

SERVES 8

Filling:

120g (8 tblsp) butter
(divide into 4 portions)
1kg beef ribeye (trimmed and
cut into 2cm cubes)
400g lambs' kidneys
(sliced and cored)
225g rindless bacon (diced)
300g (2 medium) onions
(peeled and diced)
2 cloves garlic
(peeled and chopped)
400g button mushrooms (sliced)
50g butter
50g flour
375ml (1½ cups) hot beef stock
125ml (½ cup) lager
small bunch Italian parsley
(finely chopped)
2 bayleaves
dash of Worcestershire sauce
Maldon sea salt and freshly
ground pepper

Assembly:
2 recipes Savoury Short Pastry
(see page 122)
egg wash (1 egg yolk mixed
with 1 tblsp water)

+ Preheat oven to 150°C.
+ Melt a portion of butter in a heavy frying pan and sear beef. Transfer beef to a casserole.
+ Melt a portion of butter, sear lamb kidneys and transfer kidneys to casserole.
+ Melt another portion of butter and sauté bacon, onion and garlic until soft and transfer to casserole.
+ Melt last portion of butter and sauté mushrooms until soft and transfer to casserole.
+ Using same pan make a roux by melting butter, adding flour and cooking to a sandy texture. Cool slightly, slowly add beef stock, stirring continuously. Bring sauce to the boil, add beer and bring back to the boil.
+ Continue stirring the sauce until it is thick. Add parsley, bayleaves, Worcestershire sauce and season.
+ Pour sauce over ingredients in casserole and stir to combine. Cover casserole with a lid and bake for 45–50 minutes, stirring occasionally, until beef is tender. Check for seasoning and pour into a 2.5 litre gratin dish. Allow to cool.

To assemble pie
+ Roll out one recipe of pastry, cover gratin leaving an overhang of pastry. Vent pie top. Brush egg wash on pastry top.
+ Roll out second recipe of pastry, cut 3cm-wide strips of pastry and crimp onto edges of pie top. Make pastry decorations for pie top if you wish.
+ Egg wash crimping and decorate. Trim overhang.
+ Bake at 150°C for 30 minutes or until pastry is golden brown.

Roasted Duck Breast on Potato Cake with Forest Mushroom Sauce

←

Roasted Duck Breast on Potato Cake with Forest Mushroom Sauce

Duck is absolutely perfect for a special occasion dinner. Duck and Pinot Noir are one of the classic French wine and food matches. Serve with a salad of mixed greens, and include some bitter greens in the salad to counteract the richness of the duck. Make a dressing with extra virgin olive oil and a splash of raspberry vinegar.

SERVES 6

8 duck breasts
   (trimmed of excess fat)
1 recipe Potato Cakes
1 recipe Forest Mushroom
   Sauce (see page 98)
Italian parsley for garnishing

+ Score a criss-cross pattern across skin of each duck breast (be careful as not to cut into the actual meat).
+ To sear duck breasts and to render the fat from them, heat a large frying pan to a moderate heat and without adding any oil, place duck breasts skin side down into pan.
+ Cook until skin is golden brown and crisp, pouring off duck fat.[1] Turn duck breasts over and seal on the under side. Now proceed with next step or refrigerate (even overnight) until you are ready.
+ Preheat oven to 220°C.
+ Roast seared, rendered duck breasts in a low-sided baking tray for 5–7 minutes,[2] or until medium rare. Rest covered with teatowels for at least 10 minutes to allow the juices to evenly distribute.
+ When serving, place one potato cake in the centre of each plate. Slice duck breast and place slices on top of the cake. Drizzle with Forest Mushroom Sauce and garnish with Italian parsley.

NOTE: 1. If you wish, retain the duck fat for potato cakes. 2. If seared rendered duck breasts are going into the oven from fridge allow 3–5 minutes additional cooking time.

← Golden Syrup Pudding

04 Desserts

At the end of a meal often all you want is a tiny amount of sweet – a token gesture. Make individual desserts in small containers like little soufflé dishes, demi tasse cups, shot glasses or hollowed-out limes.

If you are serving a dessert not conducive to wine – perhaps it's too citrusy, coffee flavoured or too densely chocolate – stop serving the wine, and if you want to resume alcohol serve guests a port later with coffee.

Dessert wines, dessert-style sherries and muscat liqueurs are wondrous experiences. Try serving them instead of dessert with a single matching fruit accompaniment. A glass of sauterne and a tree-ripened peach is perfect.

Custard, fruit sauces and flavoured ice-creams make interesting dessert accompaniments, but it is difficult to go past very cold, lightly whipped New Zealand cream.

Raspberries with Amaretto Cream

Amaretto is reputed to be the liqueur of love so this dessert is guaranteed to give you the perfect finale to your romantic dinner.

→
Raspberries with Amaretto Cream

SERVES 2

250g (210ml) sour cream
85g brown sugar
40ml (¼ cup) Amaretto
1 punnet raspberries

+ Place sour cream, brown sugar and Amaretto in bowl and whisk until smooth.
+ Serve raspberries generously drizzled with Amaretto cream.

Eton Mess

If you are cooking just for yourself, sometimes you need a little treat. Save the second glass of Eton Mess for when you go to bed. Pour some Amaretto over ice in a glass and enjoy with the dessert.

SERVES 2

125ml (½ cup) cream
3–4 big drops Amaretto
200g strawberries
   (hulled and chopped)
3–6 store-bought meringues
   (lightly crushed)
extra strawberries for garnish

+ Lightly beat cream and fold in liqueur to taste.
+ Fold strawberries and meringues into cream mixture.
+ Pile mixture into tall glasses and stud with extra strawberries.
+ Serve immediately.

Rata Honey Ice-cream

This ice-cream goes really well with winter fruits – feijoas macerated with sugar, nashi halves brushed with honey and roasted, apples stewed with a vanilla pod or in particular poached tamarillos. Some people tell me this is the most delicious ice-cream they have ever tasted.

SERVES 10–12

⅔ cup Rata Honey
8 egg yolks
600ml cream (lightly whipped)

+ Make an ice-cream mould by brushing a 24 x 13cm loaf tin with water and lining with plastic wrap. (If you want a smooth exterior to your ice-cream, smooth out plastic wrap wrinkles with a soft cloth).
+ Put honey into a small pot and bring to the boil. Boil for 2 minutes.
+ Put egg yolks in a bowl and begin whisking.[1] Gradually pour in hot honey, whisking continuously at high speed until the mixture has cooled. (Mixture should be whitish in colour and double its original volume.)
+ Fold the whipped cream into the egg yolk mixture and pour into the prepared mould.
+ Cover tin and freeze overnight.[2] When ready to serve unmould and slice.

NOTE: 1. I would recommend an electric mixer for this. 2. Covered in your freezer this ice-cream will keep for up to a week.

Chunky Ginger Ice-cream

I'm not sure why, but elderly people love ginger. This method of making ice-cream doesn't require churning – it is technically called a parfait.

SERVES 8–12

200g sugar
150ml water
2 vanilla beans
   (split in half lengthways)
8 egg yolks
600ml cream (lightly whipped)
30g crystallised ginger
   (chopped)

+ Put the sugar and water into a small saucepan. Scrape out vanilla bean seeds and add seeds and pods to pot. Stir over a medium-low heat until the sugar is dissolved.
+ Bring to the boil and simmer until syrup boils down to small even-sized bubbles all the way across the pot.[1]
+ Remove syrup from heat and allow to sit for 30 seconds. Remove vanilla beans (wash, dry and store for future use).
+ Put egg yolks into an electric mixer and whisk for 1 minute (of course you can whisk by hand).
+ Gradually pour on hot sugar syrup, whisking continuously.
+ Continue whisking until mixture has cooled, when it will be whitish in colour and double its original volume.
+ Fold in whipped cream and finally the ginger. Pour into a mould, cover and freeze overnight.

NOTE: 1. If you use a sugar/deep fry thermometer (easily purchased at a kitchen or hardware shop) the temperature should read 108°C–110°C.

Poached Tamarillos

←
Poached Tamarillos

Try these with muesli for breakfast or with lashings of whipped cream for dessert.

SERVES 6–12

300g sugar
750ml water
12 tamarillos
(peeled but with stalks on)[1]

+ To make a syrup, place sugar and water in a non-reactive pot and stir over a gentle heat until sugar is dissolved. Bring syrup to the boil and add tamarillos.
+ Reduce to a simmer and gently poach tamarillos for about 5 minutes. Remove pot from heat and allow tamarillos to cool in syrup. Refrigerate until required.

NOTE: 1. To peel tamarillos cut a cross at the base of the fruit, leave the stalk on, and plunge into boiling water for about 30 seconds. Remove from water, refresh gently under cold water, and remove the skin.

Citrus Salad

This is as much as you want for dessert sometimes – it is extremely refreshing.

SERVES 4–8

4 oranges
4 grapefruit (preferably pink)[1]
6 lemonades optional[2]
500ml (2 cups) water
400g (2 cups) sugar
¼ tsp cream of tartar[3]
1 tsp Grenadine[4]

NOTE: 1. Pink grapefruit are literally pink and are very sweet. They are imported from California.
2. Lemonades are very mild tasting type of lemons. I've never seen them in shops only in home gardens. They grow exceptionally well in Waikanae, on the Kapiti Coast. 3. Cream of tartar keeps the syrup clear.
4. Grenadine is a pomegranate cordial. It's delicious as a drink diluted with soda water.

+ Using a lemon zester, remove rind from one of each fruit.
+ Place zest in a non-reactive pot with water, sugar and cream of tartar.
+ Heat pot gently, stirring until sugar is dissolved. Bring liquid to the boil and simmer until thick and syrupy (it should be reduced by half. This will take approx. 20–25 minutes).
+ While syrup is simmering, remove skin and pith from fruit, and segment oranges and grapefruit (segment fruit over a bowl to catch the juice). Set fruit segments aside in bowl containing juice collected (If using lemonades cut into 4–5 slices widthways and add to bowl containing other fruit).
+ Once syrup is reduced remove from heat and add Grenadine. Allow syrup to cool for a few minutes.
+ Pour syrup over fruit and juice and stir gently to combine. Chill for at least 2 hours or overnight before serving.

Caramelised Oranges

These help to cut the richness of white Chocolate Crème Brulée – if you need it cut!
Add chopped mint to this dessert for a very cleansing finish to a meal.

SERVES 5–6

5 oranges
½ cup sugar
1 tblsp Grand Marnier
(optional)

+ Peel 4 oranges, removing all the white pith from the fruit.
+ Cut crosswise to 1cm-thick rounds, discarding the ends.
+ Squeeze juice from fifth orange and put juice into a small heavy pot.
+ Add sugar to pot.
+ On a low heat, stir juice and sugar until sugar has dissolved.
+ Increase heat to medium and, without stirring mixture, cook until it bubbles and goes golden brown.
+ Add orange rounds and swish pot around until they are covered with caramel. (The caramel may go hard on the oranges, but as the oranges sit, the caramel will return to liquid.)
+ Remove from heat, add Grand Marnier and serve when cool.

Almond Tuiles

A little biscuit always uplifts a dessert plate and gives a texture which is sometimes needed. This recipe makes 16, but just bake as many as you need and then freeze the remaining mixture.

MAKES 16 X 11CM TUILES

60g butter (softened)
60g castor sugar
50g flour
few drops vanilla essence
1½–2 egg whites
flaked almonds

+ Preheat oven to 190°C. Cream butter and sugar until light and fluffy. (We use an electric mixer).
+ Sift flour and stir in butter, sugar mixture, add vanilla essence.
+ Add enough egg white to soften mixture to a 'dropping consistency' – not liquid, but just so it falls from a spoon, or so that it could be piped from a piping bag.
+ Drop a little of the mixture onto a greased baking tray, flattening with the spoon to spread it to an 11cm circle. Sprinkle with flaked almonds.
+ Bake for 5–6 minutes or until the edges of the tuiles are light brown and the centres are cooked through.
+ Remove tray from oven and drape tuiles over the curve of a rolling pin. Once cold, store what you require in an airtight container and then freeze the rest.

White Chocolate Crème Brulée

Michael Lee-Richards, Christchurch chef and cooking teacher, started us off on White Chocolate Crème Brulée. It is one of our top-selling desserts. You need a good quality white chocolate. We use a Belgian chocolate. You can of course substitute dark chocolate for white chocolate, but it's somehow not as good.

SERVES 5

5 egg yolks
110g (½ cup) sugar plus 5 tsp
  for sprinkling over brulées
500ml (2 cups) cream
½ vanilla bean
  (split in half lengthways)
75g white chocolate
  (or buttons finely chopped)

+ Preheat oven to 150ºC. Whisk egg yolks with half the sugar in a medium bowl until combined.
+ Pour the cream into a saucepan and add the remaining sugar. Scrape seeds from vanilla bean and add seeds and bean to cream. Over a low heat, stir until sugar is dissolved. Bring to the boil, then reduce heat to low.
+ Add white chocolate to cream mixture and whisk until smooth.
+ Gradually and slowly whisk hot chocolate mixture into yolk mixture. Aim for a 'no froth' mixture. If froth forms, then scoop it off before you do next step.
+ Pour the custard into 5 individual soufflé dishes or ovenproof espresso cups and place into a roasting tray. Add enough hot water to roasting tray to come halfway up the sides of soufflé dishes.
+ Bake for 55–60 minutes or until the custards are just set in the centre. Remove from the water and cool. Cover and refrigerate overnight.

To serve
+ Sprinkle 1 tsp sugar over each custard and torch or grill until the sugar caramelises. Serve immediately.

Muscat-poached Fruit on Brioche with Mascarpone

←
Muscat-poached
Fruit on Brioche
with Mascarpone

You can serve this fruit on store-bought sponge cake. Make a big quantity of fruit and store in fridge to serve with ice-cream.

SERVES 4–6

1 loaf brioche bread[1]
½ recipe Muscat-poached Fruit
    (below)
mascarpone[2]

+ Slice 4–6 slices of bread and cut into rounds using a 6.5cm cookie cutter. Toast.
+ To serve, place 3–4 pieces of fruit onto brioche with some of the syrup and serve with mascarpone.

NOTE: 1. You can buy brioche bread at a French bakery. Freeze the rest of the loaf sliced and cut into rounds for next time. Toast the brioche if it comes out of the freezer. 2. Mascarpone cheese is a buttery-rich, creamy cheese made from cow's milk. It's yummy sweetened and served as an accompaniment with fruit.

Muscat-poached Fruit

SERVES 12–15

750ml (3 cups) muscat
1 cup water
2½ cups castor sugar
1 vanilla bean (split in half)
165g (10) tenderised figs
85g (12) dried apricots
35g (8) pitted prunes
135g (10) dried peaches
130g (10) dried pear halves

+ In a heavy-based saucepan, bring muscat, water, castor sugar and vanilla bean to the boil over a high heat, stirring to dissolve sugar. Reduce heat and simmer for 20 minutes until liquid begins to thicken and becomes syrupy.
+ Add fruit and simmer for 20 minutes until fruit is tender and syrup has reduced. Remove vanilla bean.
+ Use warm, or store until required.
+ Keep any left-over syrup to soak currants and raisins.

Hazelnut Dacquoise with Whipped Cream, Chocolate Sauce and Apricot Compote

A very Cordon Bleu dessert, actually done to death, but everyone loves it. Great to cook because you can make the dacquoise a good 5 days ahead. Do not store in airtight container!

→

**Hazelnut Dacquoise
with Whipped Cream,
Chocolate Sauce and
Apricot Compote**

SERVES 8–10

125g (1 cup) hazelnuts
4 (½ cup) egg whites
½ tsp cream of tartar
250g (1¼ cups) castor sugar
8g (1 tblsp) cocoa
1 tsp vanilla essence
whipped cream
1 recipe Chocolate Sauce
   (see page 116)
1 recipe Apricot Compote
   (see page 116)

+ Preheat oven to 180°C. Line a baking tray with baking paper. Draw two 20cm circles on the paper.
+ Roast hazelnuts for 5–7 minutes or until skins begin to flake off. Roughly remove skins and grind hazelnuts in a food processor fitted with a metal blade.
+ Reduce oven temperature to 130°C. Whisk egg whites with cream of tartar in large bowl until whites begin to stiffen (at this stage think frothy rather than stiff).
+ Add half of the sugar and whisk until shiny.
+ Sift remaining sugar with cocoa. Fold into egg white mixture with ground hazelnuts and vanilla.
+ Spoon mixture onto circles and gently smooth out to fill circles. Bake for 1–1¼ hours or until firm.
+ Remove from oven. Leave for 2–3 hours before serving or better still overnight.

To serve
+ Place one circle of Hazelnut Dacquoise onto a platter and cover with a generous amount of whipped cream. Place a second circle on top and drizzle with hot Chocolate Sauce. Serve with Apricot Compote.[1]

Note: 1. In summer serve with fresh raspberries rather than Apricot Compote.

Chocolate Sauce

During the peak of strawberry season serve this sauce hot with the ripest, biggest strawberries and vanilla ice-cream.

125ml cream
125g dark chocolate

+ Place cream in a saucepan and bring to the boil. Remove from heat and add chocolate.
+ Stir until chocolate is completely melted.

Apricot Compote

Make extra and store in the fridge to have on hand to serve warm with ice-cream or with muesli for breakfast.

SERVES 10

20 dried apricots (the bigger
   and juicier the better – I like
   dried apricots from Otago)
hot water to cover
300g (1½ cups) castor sugar
1 litre (4 cups) water
1 vanilla bean
   (split lengthways) (optional)

+ Soak the apricots in hot water for at least 1 hour.
+ Bring sugar, water (and vanilla bean) to the boil, stirring to dissolve sugar. Add drained apricots and simmer for 15 minutes or until apricots are soft.

Poached Pears with Passionfruit

Lovely as an accompaniment to puddings or as a dessert on its own with a glass of sticky wine.

SERVES 4

4 small firm pears
  (Packham Triumphs are
  great for poaching)
juice of 1 lemon
125ml (½ cup) passionfruit pulp
375ml (1½ cups) water
300g (1¼ cups) sugar

+ Peel pears but leave stalks on. Place in additional water with lemon juice until you are ready to poach them.
+ Put passionfruit pulp, water and sugar in a pot and stir until sugar is dissolved. Bring to the boil.
+ Add pears, bring syrup back to boil and then reduce to a simmer.
+ Cover syrup with a piece of baking paper so pears stay submerged.
+ Simmer pears until tender right through. This could take up to an hour but depends on ripeness of pears. Serve hot, warm or cold.

Orange Crème Anglaise

A must with Golden Syrup Puddings (below). Yes, you still need to serve whipped cream.

SERVES 10

150ml cream
150ml milk
zest of 2 oranges
3 egg yolks
65g (⅓ cup) castor sugar

NOTE: Orange Crème Anglaise may be served warm or cold.

+ Pour cream and milk in a non-reactive pot. Add orange zest and bring to the boil. Remove cream mixture from heat and leave to steep for 2 hours.
+ Reheat cream mixture. Whisk egg yolks and sugar until pale and thick. Slowly pour on the hot cream mixture whisking continuously.
+ Return mixture to saucepan and over a low heat, stirring continuously, cook until mixture begins to thicken. The custard should be thick enough to coat a spoon.
+ Strain Orange Crème Anglaise into a bowl and serve.

Golden Syrup Puddings

If you want to eat puddings the next day leave in moulds, store at room temperature rather than in the fridge and reheat at 190°C in an oven dish with hot water one-third of the way up the moulds.

→
**Golden Syrup Pudding
with whipped cream**

SERVES 10

200g (1 cup) sticky raisins[1]
juice of 4 oranges (warmed)
10 tblsp golden syrup
   (or more if you are going to
   reheat puddings)
100g butter (cubed and at
   room temperature)
110g (½ cup firmly packed)
   brown sugar
2 eggs
280g (2 cups) flour
1 tsp baking powder
¼ tsp salt
zest of 1 orange
125ml (½ cup) milk

+ Preheat oven to 190ºC.
+ Soak raisins in orange juice for 30 minutes. Drain and reserve juice for another use.
+ Spray or grease 10 dariole moulds (6.5cm diameter).[2] Divide golden syrup between moulds.
+ Cream butter and sugar until light and fluffy. Add eggs, one at a time, beating continuously.
+ Sift flour, baking powder and salt and gently fold into butter mixture. Add raisins and zest.
+ Add milk and fold into batter mixture.
+ Divide batter mixture between moulds.
+ Place moulds into an oven dish and add boiling water to come one-third of the way up the moulds.
+ Cover oven dish with tinfoil and bake for 30-35 minutes or until a skewer comes out clean.
+ Gently shake puddings out of the moulds and serve.

NOTE: 1. We use Lexia which are the old-fashioned sticky raisins.
2. You could use small ramekins or espresso cups.

Old-fashioned Apple Pie

Apple Pie is still one of our most popular desserts. We often make individual versions of this recipe.

→
Old-fashioned Apple Pie

SERVES 8–10

1 recipe Sweet Short Pastry
  (see page 122)
about 1.8kg (12 medium
  apples)[1] peeled and thinly
  sliced
juice of 2 lemons
zest of 2 lemons
zest of 1 orange
5 tblsp flour
pinch ground cloves
½ tsp cinnamon
¾–1 cup brown sugar
  (depending on sweetness
  of apples)
2 tblsp finely diced butter
1 egg white (slightly whisked)
1 egg yolk (lightly beaten with
  1 tblsp cold water)

+ Lightly grease, or spray with baking spray, a 30cm metal pie dish with removable base.
+ Roll out pastry to fit base leaving an overhang around pie dish. You will have some pastry left. Rest pie base in fridge for at least 30 minutes.
+ Preheat oven to 200°C.
+ For the pie top use a cookie cutter to cut shapes out of remaining pastry. Place shapes in fridge until ready to use. (We use heart cutters.)
+ To make filling toss apples, lemon juice and zests, flour, spices, brown sugar and butter together.
+ Brush pie base with egg white[2] and place filling in base. Fold in pastry overhang to form a double edge and crimp.
+ Glaze shapes with egg yolk and place on pie.
+ Bake pie for 10 minutes and then reduce oven to 180°C for 1–1½ hours, or until apple is cooked and pie is golden and bubbly.[3]
+ Serve hot or warm with vanilla ice-cream and whipped cream.

NOTE: 1. Preferably Braeburn apples as they keep their shape when cooked. 2. This helps seal the pastry. 3. Place pie dish on a baking tray so that bubbling juices won't soil your oven.

Baby Florentines

We keep a permanent supply of these iced in the freezer to serve with coffee instead of dessert.

MAKES 40 X 3CM DIAMETER BISCUITS

170g butter
100g (½ cup) sugar
45ml (3 tblsp) cream
60g (⅓ cup) glacé cherries
   (chopped)
140g (1¼ cups) flaked almonds
85g (½ cup) mixed peel
30g (2 tblsp) flour
230g dark chocolate

+ Preheat oven to 180°C. Put butter, sugar and cream in a small, heavy-bottomed saucepan. Stir and bring to the boil.
+ Add cherries, almonds, mixed peel and flour. Stir and remove from heat.
+ Drop small teaspoonfuls of mixture on a sprayed baking tray (no more than 8 biscuits on one tray).
+ Cook for 5–7 minutes or until biscuits are brown around the edges.
+ Remove biscuits from oven and shape into rounds using a cookie cutter. When biscuits are cool, remove from tray.
+ Melt chocolate and spread on bottom side of each biscuit. Allow to set, store in an airtight container.

Sweet Short Pastry

A good basic pastry for many desserts.

210g (1½ cups) flour
½ tsp salt
45g (3 tblsp) sugar[1]
100g cold unsalted butter
   (diced)
1 egg yolk
45ml (3 tblsp) very cold water
   (approx.)

+ With a metal blade in food processor, place flour, salt and sugar in food processor bowl.
+ Sprinkle butter over flour and process until mixture looks like fine breadcrumbs.
+ In a small bowl, whisk egg yolk with cold water.
+ With food processor running, pour egg yolk mixture through feed tube. Continue to process until the pastry forms a ball.
+ If the pastry does not form a ball easily, remove mixture from food processor and finish the balling process with your hands. Form pastry into a disc, plastic wrap and rest in fridge for at least 30 minutes before using.[2]

NOTE: 1. Substitute sugar for ½ tsp salt and a grind of black pepper and you will have Savoury Short Pastry. 2. You can freeze this pastry.

Homemade Old-fashioned Jam Tarts

Strawberry jam that still has whole strawberries in it works well in these tarts, or a tart jam like plum. Handy to pack these tarts into a picnic lunch.

TO MAKE 10 TARTS

500g puff or flaky pastry[1]
1½ cups homemade jam
egg glaze
castor sugar

+ Roll out pastry and using a saucer or similar as a template cut into 16cm rounds.
+ Place pastry in foil pie dishes[2] (pastry will be hanging over the edges). Let pastry rest for at least 30 minutes.
+ Preheat oven to 220°C.
+ Place a generous dessertspoon of jam into each pie base.
+ Bring the edges of pastry in towards the centre, leaving the centre uncovered. Crimp the edges.
+ Brush the crimping with egg glaze and sprinkle with castor sugar.
+ Bake for 10 minutes and then reduce oven to 200°C for a further 5 minutes or until tart is golden brown.

NOTE: 1. We use a good quailty commerical puff pastry. 2. You can buy these at supermarkets, 10cm is the top measurement.

Tiramisu

This is an Italian 'pick me up'. Very alcohol and caffeine rich.

MAKES 8–12 SERVES

50g (¼ cup) castor sugar
300ml strong black coffee (hot)
125ml (½ cup) Scotch whiskey
175g sponge fingers, cut in
   half on the bias
4 eggs
100g (½ cup) castor sugar
500g mascarpone cheese
190ml (¾ cup) Marsala
80g dark chocolate for grating

+ Dissolve castor sugar in coffee and whiskey. Chill.
+ Briefly dip sponge fingers into coffee mixture one at a time and arrange 3 pieces of sponge fingers into the bottom of each serving glass.
+ Whisk eggs with second measure of castor sugar until stiff and white. Whisk together mascarpone and marsala.
+ Using a metal spoon, gently combine the egg mixture with the mascarpone mixture.
+ Place two dessertspoons of mascarpone mixture over the sponge fingers and cover with a thin layer of grated dark chocolate. Repeat the layers of mascarpone mixture and chocolate.
+ Chill for at least 6 hours or overnight.

→
Martini glasses of Tiramisu in ice in a buffet

Marble Bark

MAKES ABOUT 80 PIECES

150g (1 cup) almonds
   (blanched)
135g (1 cup) hazelnuts
500g white chocolate
500g dark chocolate

+ Roast almonds and hazelnuts in a 180°C oven until golden.
+ Remove hazelnut skins and coarsely chop nuts.
+ In separate bowls gently melt white chocolate and dark chocolate.
+ Stir ½ cup of almonds and ½ cup of hazelnuts into white chocolate and the remainder into the dark chocolate.
+ Spray a sponge roll tin with baking spray.
+ Alternating the white and dark chocolate, spoon melted chocolate into tin (chocolate should be ¾–1cm thick when finished).
+ Let chocolate cool slightly then run a knife through it to obtain a marbled effect.
+ Refrigerate until firm, remove from tin, and smash into irregular pieces.

INDEX